James Lombard

A Liturgy with a Collection of Hymns and Chants

For the Use of Sunday Schools

James Lombard

A Liturgy with a Collection of Hymns and Chants
For the Use of Sunday Schools

ISBN/EAN: 9783337082536

Printed in Europe, USA, Canada, Australia, Japan

Cover: Foto ©Paul-Georg Meister /pixelio.de

More available books at **www.hansebooks.com**

A

LITURGY,

WITH A COLLECTION OF

HYMNS AND CHANTS,

FOR

THE USE OF SUNDAY SCHOOLS.

―――――

BY JAMES LOMBARD.

―――――

"Lord, teach us to pray."

BOSTON:

PUBLISHED BY ABEL TOMPKINS,

38 & 40 Cornhill.

1860.

PREFACE.

THE want of a Ritual, at once simple, direct and impressive, has long been felt by those connected with Sunday Schools. This little volume has been prepared to meet that want. If the object the author aims to secure, be attained, he will feel amply rewarded for his labor.

This LITURGY is designed to be used in the following manner:

At the opening of the School, after the Superintendent or leader of the devotions, shall have read the first part of the introductory sentence, and the teachers and children the succeeding part, the Superintendent will then read the EXHORTATION. The brief prayer following, together with the LORD'S PRAYER, will be said in concert by all present.

The PSALMS or RESPONSES, will be read alternately by the Superintendent, and the teachers and children together.

When a short SCRIPTURAL LESSON is read, it should follow the PSALM.

The longer PRAYER preceding the CLASS LESSONS, is designed to be read in distinct passages, as indicated by the marks of separation. Each passage to be read first by the Superintendent alone, and then repeated by the teachers and children together.

The CONCLUDING PRAYER should be read by the Superintendent only, at the close of the School.

By observing this simple form, order, dignity and impressiveness will mark the devotional exercises of the School.

Those who would secure the best results, should adopt one service, and adhere to it, varying the Psalms and Prayers, only when occasion requires. In this way the children will become familiar with the service, and learn to love it. Experience has deepened the author's conviction that one "form of sound words" is a better devotional exercise than varied spontaneous utterances, however excellent. It more easily engages the attention, especially of the young, and seldom fails to inspire a feeling of devotion.

For important suggestions in preparing the work the author is indebted to many valued friends, and also to eminent divines, who have most cordially approved his labors.

In collecting and arranging the Hymns, he is happy to express his indebtedness to Mrs. Sawyer, Mrs. E. Oakes Smith, Mrs. Sigourney, Alice Cary and Grace Greenwood, Revs. R. C. Waterston, C. T. Brooks and John Pierpont, and Messrs. Theodore Tilton, R. F. Fuller, and W. C. Bryant.

The Hymns marked with an asterisk, are either original, or revised and furnished by the authors for this work. These are protected by the copyright.

UTICA, OCTOBER 1st, 1859.

INDEX.

/

I.

OFFICE OF DEVOTION

AT THE

OPENING OF THE SCHOOL.

———•◆•———

Superintendent. — It is a good thing to give thanks unto the Lord,

Children. — And to sing praises unto Thy name, O, Most High.

———

THE EXHORTATION.

DEAR CHILDREN, — It is right that we should thank God for all the good gifts that we receive at His hands. And though we ought at all times to praise Him for His great love, yet ought we more so to do when we meet to worship in His holy temple.

It is His will that we should love Him; and if we love Him with our whole heart, we

9

shall keep His laws, and walk in His ways.
And now, that we are come to draw near to
God, let us ask Him to draw near to us.
And while we think of Him, and call upon
His name, may we feel that He hears us, and
will grant us more than we can ask or think.
To this end, I pray you who are now here,
to join me with a pure heart and humble
voice, at the throne of grace, saying,—

WE thank Thee, our Father, that Thou
hast given us Thy word,— and that we
are taught Thy truth. — May we learn to
love that truth. — May it be so fixed in
our minds,—that, with the faith of Christ on
our lips, and in our hearts, — we may know
and do Thy will. — So shall our tongues
praise Thee with songs of joy,—and our hearts
shall love Thee more than words can tell.

Be with us now that we are here to bless
Thy name : — Be with us at all times. — Blot
out all our sins,— and make us to serve Thee
now and ever more — through Jesus Christ
our Lord. *Amen.*

OUR Father who art in Heaven, Hallowed
be Thy name ; Thy kingdom come ; Thy
will be done on earth as it is in Heaven ;
Give us this day our daily bread ; and forgive us our trespasses as we forgive those
who trespass against us ; And lead us not
into temptation ; but deliver us from evil ;
For Thine is the kingdom, and the power,
and the glory, for ever and ever. *Amen.*

Supt. — O Lord open Thou our lips ;

Chil. — And our mouth shall show forth Thy praise.

[Then shall be said, all standing, alternately by the Superintendent and Children, the following]

PSALM.

From Psalms xcv., xcvi.

Supt. — O come let us sing unto the Lord,

Chil. — Let us heartily rejoice in the strength of our salvation.

Supt. — Let us come before His presence with thanksgiving,

Chil. — And show ourselves glad in Him with psalms.

Supt. — For the Lord is a great God ;

Chil. — And a great King above all gods.

Supt. — In His hand are all the corners of the earth,

Chil. — And the strength of the hills is His also.

Supt. — The sea is His, and He made it ;

Chil. — And His hands prepared the dry land.

Supt. — O come let us worship, and fall down,

Chil. — And kneel before the Lord our Maker.

Supt. — For He is the Lord our God ;

Chil. — And we are the people of His pasture, and the sheep of His hand.

Supt. — O worship the Lord in the beauty of holiness;

Chil. — Let the whole earth stand in awe of Him,

Supt. — For He cometh,

Chil. — For He cometh to judge the earth ;

Supt. — And with righteousness to judge the world,

Chil. — And the people with His truth.

[The Superintendent shall then say, the Children repeating after him, this]

PRAYER.

WE praise Thee, O God,—we own Thee to be the Lord : — Thou art the light and life of all things. — All the world gives praise to Thee, — for Thou only art good.

We bless Thee, O God, that Thou art our Father, — and we are Thy children — and that Thou hast taught us to serve Thee with glad hearts.

Thou hast breathed into us the breath of life. — Thou hast given light to our minds, — joy to our hearts, — and health and strength to our bodies. — Thou hast given us friends to love us, — and Teachers to show us how to be wise and good.

We thank Thee, Father, for these Thy gifts, — and pray that we may use them in the right way. — But more than all, we thank Thee — that Thou hast sent Thy son, — to

teach us the way Thou wouldst have us go.
— May His great love draw us to Thee more
and more. — May the truth He taught take
deep root in our hearts and minds, — and
bring forth in our lives the fruit of joy and
peace.

We pray Thee, O Lord, to bless our
School, — May it be our chief joy here to
learn how great and good Thou art. — And
when we cease to thank Thee on earth ; —
take us to Thyself — that we may praise Thee
in a world that shall have no end, — through
Jesus Christ our Lord. *Amen.*

CLOSING PRAYER.

OUR Father, let not our worship cease
with our words, — but may our whole
life be one gift of thanks for Thy great love.
— May we do Thy will as our best sacrifice.
— May we yield our hearts to Thee as our
best praise. — And when the service of life
shall end, — may we give Thee purer worship in Heaven. — Forgive all our sins, — and
may we, from this time forth, feel that we are
not alone, — for Thou, our God, art with us,
— through Jesus Christ our Lord. *Amen.*

BENEDICTION.

The grace of the Lord Jesus Christ be
with you all. *Amen.*

II.

OFFICE OF DEVOTION

AT THE

OPENING OF THE SCHOOL.

———•••———

Supt. —This is none other but the house
of God ;
Chil. — And this is the gate of Heaven.

———

THE EXHORTATION.

DEAR CHILDREN, — We are come to praise
God in this His house, to hear His word of
truth, and to learn the way of life. We
should feel that God is here, and that He
reads the thoughts of our minds, and knows
all that is in our hearts. And now, that we
are come before Him, let us have none but
pure thoughts and feelings. Let us feel that
He is our Father, and look up to Him as
children, with full trust in His love. His
eye is upon us, but it is the eye of a Father,

14

who would have us do what is right, that
we may be happy. Let us not take His
name upon our lips, while our hearts are far
from Him. But when we pray to Him to
bless us, let us ask in such wise that we may
hope to be filled with His peace.

To this end I pray you who are now here,
to join me with a pure heart and humble
voice, at the throne of grace, saying,

FATHER in Heaven, we cannot sin against
Thee and not suffer. — We cannot stray
from Thee and not be lost. — We cannot hate
the light, and not wrong our own souls. — We
need light, and Thou alone canst give it. —
We are weak, and Thou alone canst make us
strong. — Help us that we may walk in the
light — and have strength to do Thy will —
through Jesus Christ our Lord. *Amen.*

OUR Father who art in Heaven, Hallowed
be Thy name ; Thy kingdom come ; Thy
will be done on earth as it is in Heaven;
Give us this day our daily bread ; and forgive us our trespasses as we forgive those
who trespass against us ; And lead us not
into temptation ; but deliver us from evil ;
For Thine is the kingdom, and the power,
and the glory, for ever and ever. *Amen.*

Supt. — O Lord, open Thou our lips ;
Chil. — And our mouth shall show forth
Thy praise.

[Then shall be said, all standing, alternately by the Superintendent and Children, the following]

P S A L M.

Psalm lxvii.

Supt. — God be merciful unto us, and bless us,

Chil. — And show us the light of His countenance,

Supt. — And be merciful unto us;

Chil. — That Thy way may be known upon earth,

Supt. — Thy saving health among all nations.

Chil. — Let the people praise Thee, O God;

Supt. — Yea, let all the people praise Thee.

Chil. — O let the nations rejoice and be glad ;

Supt. — For Thou shalt judge the people righteously,

Chil. — And govern the nations upon earth.

Supt. — Let the people praise Thee, O God ;

Chil. — Yea, let all the people praise Thee.

Supt. — Then shall the earth bring forth her increase ;

Chil. — And God, even our own God, shall give us His blessing.

Supt. — God shall bless us;

Chil. — And all the ends of the world shall fear Him.

[The Superintendent shall then say, the Children repeating after him, this]

PRAYER.

FATHER in Heaven, we mourn Thou hast been so little in our thoughts. — We grieve that we honor Thee so little in our lives. — Day after day we say that we will sin no more : — But our hearts go back, and we find that all our strength is weakness. — It is in vain that we say we thank Thee,—since our lives, which speak so much louder than our words, — show that we do not thank Thee as we ought. — Let us mock Thee no more, and thus cheat our own souls. — Let us not confess our sins with our lips, — while we cleave to them with our hearts. — Better were it for us to leave our prayers unsaid, — than to take words upon our lips in which our hearts have no share. — O Lord, may we ever bear in mind — how sad a thing is sin. —Thou art the Way the Truth and the Life.— Be Thou ever with us, — to make clean our hands, — to make pure our lips, — to guard our thoughts, — and to make right all our ways. — We ask it through Jesus Christ our Lord. *Amen.*

CLOSING PRAYER.

FATHER in Heaven,—grant that the words which we have heard this day with our ears,—may bring forth in our hearts the fruit of a good life.

We pray Thee to go with us from this place,—and to bless us.—Keep us from all harm in the time to come.—May our hearts be stayed on Thee in every grief we bear.— Lead us safe through all the scenes of life.— And when with us this world shall cease,— take us to that Heaven of peace and joy,— which shall have no end ;—through Jesus Christ our Lord. *Amen.*

BENEDICTION.

The Lord of peace go with you, and may you find peace now, and always. *Amen.*

III.

OFFICE OF DEVOTION

OPENING OF THE SCHOOL.

Supt. — The Lord is in His holy temple ;
Chil. — Let all the earth keep silence before Him.

THE EXHORTATION.

DEAR CHILDREN, — We are met to learn those truths which will make us wise and save us from sin. We ought to come with meek hearts and right minds. We ought to come in the love of God, and with full trust in His mercy. He made us and all things. He has been with us, and blest us since the first day of our life. He is our Father in Heaven. We are his children. We ought

to love Him, for He first loved us. He is
good, and all His works are good. Even
when we do wrong, He shows us the·path of
light and truth.

And now, that we are come to thank Him
for all the joys of life, and to bless His holy
name, let us bear in mind that He is here
with us, and that all our thoughts, and words,
and deeds, are known to Him. Let us look
to Him for the help we need. Let us confess
our sins to Him, and ask Him to take them
away. To this end I pray you who are now
here, to join me with a pure heart and
humble voice, at the throne of grace, saying, —

CONFESSION.

MOST High and Holy God ; We have
erred and strayed from Thy ways like
lost sheep.—We have gone too much in the
way of our own hearts.—We have sinned
against Thy holy laws.—We have not done
those things we ought to have done,—and we
have done those things which we ought not
to have done.—And all our help is in Thee.—
We are weak and need Thine aid.—Grant us
Thy Peace, that we may walk in the light.—
We pray Thee to forgive all our sins.—And
grant, that from this time forth we may serve
Thee all the days of our life,—through Jesus
Christ our Lord.—As Thy Son, O God, has
taught us, we would pray :

OUR Father who art in Heaven, Hallowed be Thy name ; Thy kingdom come ; Thy will be done on earth as it is in Heaven ; Give us this day our daily bread ; and forgive us our trespasses as we forgive those who trespass against us ; And lead us not into temptation ; but deliver us from evil ; For Thine is the kingdom, and the power, and the glory, for ever and ever. *Amen.*

Supt. — O Lord, open Thou our lips ;
Chil. — And our mouth shall show forth Thy praise.

[Then shall be said, all standing, alternately by the Superintendent and Children, the following]

PSALM.

Supt. — Praise the Lord, O my soul ;
Chil. — And all that is within me, praise His holy name.
Supt. — Praise the Lord, O my soul,
Chil. — And forget not all His benefits :
Supt. — Who forgiveth all thy sin,
Chil. — And healeth all thine infirmities ;
Supt. — Who saveth thy life from destruction,
Chil. — And crowneth thee with mercy and loving-kindness.
Supt. — O praise the Lord, ye Angels of His, ye that excel in strength ;

Chil. — Ye that fulfil His commandments, and hearken unto the voice of His word.

Supt. — O praise the Lord, all ye His hosts ;

Chil. — Ye servants of His that do His pleasure.

Supt. — O speak good of the Lord, all ye works of His, in all places of His dominion :

Chil. — Praise thou the Lord, O my soul.

[The Superintendent shall then say, the Children repeating after him, this]

PRAYER.

OUR Father, in whom are light and life and all things, — fill our hearts, with a sense of Thy love. — Teach us to serve Thee as we ought. — Grant us the aid of Thy grace — that we may know and do Thy will. — So shall we dwell in the light of Thy truth, — and Thou wilt be with us, — and Thy right hand shall lead us — all the days of our life.

We thank Thee for health and strength, — and for all the blessings of this life. — But more than all we bless Thee for the gift of Thy Son, — for the light of Thy word, — and for the hope of the life to come.

May we show forth Thy praise, O Lord, — not with our lips alone, — but in our lives. — Make us to know Thy truth. — Thy word is truth. — Write that word upon our hearts, —

that we may have Thee always in our thoughts.—Teach us to love Thee with pure hearts, —with all our mind, might and strength.

Thou didst send Thy Son to take away the sin of the world. — Blot out all our sins, O God, — and make us Thine, in will and deed, — through Jesus Christ our Lord. *Amen.*

CLOSING PRAYER.

WE pray Thee, O Lord, to bless our School.—Grant Thine aid to those who teach,—that they may find joy in the work they have to do.—Bless these children.—May the right means be used to teach them Thy truth.—Be Thou their guard and guide,—and show them the way in which they should go.

By Thee, O God, all hearts are seen,—all wants are known.—From Thee no thought or word is hid.—May it please Thee to cleanse the thoughts of our hearts,—that we may love Thee in truth,—and live to the praise of Thy name, — through Jesus Christ our Lord. *Amen.*

BENEDICTION.

The Lord go with you, and may you find grace in His sight.

[This may be used in place of the Opening Prayer, at the discretion of the Superintendent.]

LITANY.

O God, of whom, through whom, and to whom are all things,

May it please Thee to bless the whole world, and give all the nations peace ;

We pray Thee to hear us, our Father.

May it please Thee to bless the land in which we live ;

We pray Thee to hear us, our Father.

May it please Thee to bless those who are called to rule our land ;

We pray Thee to hear us, our Father.

May it please Thee to be with the Pastor of this Church, in all his work, that he may not fear to set forth Thy holy word ;

We pray Thee to hear us, our Father.

May it please Thee to bless all who are sick, or in any kind of trouble, to give them peace, and send them help in their time of need ;

We pray Thee to hear us, our Father.

May it please Thee to bless the poor, that they may be fed and clothed, and learn the way of life ;

We pray Thee to hear us, our Father.

May it please Thee to bring back to Thy flock all who walk in the way of sin, and to keep them in Thy fold ;

We pray Thee to hear us, our Father.

May it please Thee to bless our friends, to give them health and joy, that they may live in Thy light;

We pray Thee to hear us, our Father.

May it please Thee to bless us, even us, to give us true faith, to take away our sins, and fill us with Thy love;

We pray Thee to hear us, our Father.

O Lord, bless us and keep us; O Lord, make Thy face to shine upon us, and grant us Thy peace, now and ever more.

O Lord, bless us and keep us; O Lord, make Thy face to shine upon us, and grant us Thy peace now and ever more.

ADDITIONAL PSALMS.

I

From Psalm xix.

Supt. — The law of the Lord is perfect,

Chil. — Converting the soul:

Supt. — The testimony of the Lord is sure,

Chil. — Making wise the simple:

Supt. — The statutes of the Lord are right,

Chil. — Rejoicing the heart:

Supt. — The commandment of the Lord is pure,

Chil. — Enlightening the eyes.

Supt. — The fear of the Lord is clean,

Chil. — Enduring forever:

Supt. — The judgments of the Lord are true and righteous altogether.

Chil. — More to be desired are they than gold,

Supt. — Yea, than much fine gold :

Chil. — Sweeter also than honey, and the honey-comb.

Supt. — Moreover by them is thy servant taught ;

Chil.— And in keeping of them is great reward.

Supt. — Who can understand his errors ?

Chil. — O cleanse Thou me from secret faults.

Supt. — Keep Thy servant also from presumptuous sins ;

Chil. — Let them not have dominion over me :

Supt. — Then shall I be upright,

Chil.— And I shall be innocent from the great transgression.

Supt. — Let the words of my mouth,

Chil. — And the meditation of my heart,

Supt. — Be always acceptable in Thy sight,

Chil. — O Lord, my strength and my Redeemer.

II.

From Psalm xxiv.

Supt. — The earth is the Lord's, and the fullness thereof ;

Chil. — The world, and they that dwell therein.

Supt. — For He hath founded it upon the seas,

Chil. — And prepared it upon the floods.

Supt. — Who shall ascend into the hill of the Lord ?

Chil. — Or who shall stand in His holy place ?

Supt. — He that hath clean hands, and a pure heart ;

Chil. — Who hath not lifted up his soul unto vanity, nor sworn deceitfully,

Supt. — He shall receive the blessing from the Lord,

Chil. — And righteousness from the God of his salvation.

Supt. — Lift up your heads, O ye gates ;

Chil. — And be ye lifted up, ye everlasting doors ;

Supt. — And the King of glory shall come in.

Chil. — Who is this King of glory ?

Supt. — The Lord strong and mighty, the Lord mighty in battle.

Chil. — Lift up your heads, O ye gates ;

Supt. — Even lift them up, ye everlasting doors ;

Chil. — And the King of glory shall come in.

Supt. — Who is this King of glory ?

Chil. — The Lord of hosts, He is the King of glory.

III.

From Psalm xxxiv.

Supt. — I will bless the Lord at all times :

Chil. — His praise shall ever be in my mouth.

Supt. — My soul shall make her boast in the Lord :

Chil. — The humble shall hear thereof, and be glad.

Supt. — O magnify the Lord with me,

Chil. — And let us praise His name together.

Supt. — O taste and see that the Lord is good :

Chil. — Blessed is the man that trusteth in Him.

Supt. — O fear the Lord, ye that are His saints :

Chil. — For they that fear Him lack nothing.

Supt. — Come, ye children, and hearken unto me ;

Chil. — And I will teach you the fear of the Lord.

Supt. — What man is he that desireth life,

Chil. — And loveth many days, that he may see good ?

Supt. — Keep thy tongue from evil,

Chil. — And thy lips from speaking guile.

Supt. — Depart from evil, and do good ;

Chil. — Seek peace, and pursue it.

Supt. — The Lord is nigh unto them that are of a broken heart ;

Chil. — And will save such as be of an humble spirit.

Supt. — Great are the troubles of the righteous ;

Chil. — But the Lord delivereth him out of them all.

Supt. — The Lord redeemeth the souls of his servants ;

Chil. — And none of them that trust in Him shall be desolate.

IV.
From Psalm xcii.

Supt. — It is a good thing to give thanks unto the Lord,

Chil. — And to sing praises unto Thy name, O Most High :

Supt. — To tell of Thy loving-kindness early in the morning,

Chil. — And of Thy truth in the night-season,

Supt. — Upon an instrument of ten strings, and upon the lute ;

Chil. — Upon a loud instrument, and upon the harp:

Supt. — For Thou, Lord, hast made me glad through Thy work,

Chil. — And I will triumph in the works of Thy hands.

Supt. — O Lord, how great are Thy works ;

Chil. — And Thy thoughts are very deep.

Supt. — An unwise man knoweth not ;

Chil. — Neither doth a fool understand this.

Supt. — The righteous shall flourish like the palm-tree :

Chil. — He shall grow like a cedar in Lebanon.

Supt. — Those that he planted in the house of the Lord,

Chil. — Shall flourish in the courts of our God ;

Supt. — That they may show how true the Lord my strength is,

Chil. — And that there is no unrighteousness in Him.

V.

Psalm xcviii.

Supt. — O sing unto the Lord a new song ;

Chil. — For He hath done marvellous things.

Supt. — With His own right hand, and with His holy arm,

Chil. — Hath He gotten Himself the victory.

Supt. — The Lord declared His salvation ;

Chil. — His righteousness hath He openly showed in the sight of the heathen.

Supt. — He hath remembered His mercy and truth toward the house of Israel,

Chil. — And all the ends of the world have seen the salvation of our God.

Supt. — Show yourselves joyful unto the Lord, all ye lands ;

Chil. — Sing, rejoice, and give thanks

Supt. — Praise the Lord upon the harp ;

Chil. — Sing to the harp with a psalm of thanksgiving.

Supt. — With trumpets also, and shawms,

Chil. — O show yourselves joyful before the Lord the King.

Supt. — Let the sea make a noise, and all that therein is ;

Chil. — The round world, and they that dwell therein.

Supt. — Let the floods clap their hands,

and let the hills be joyful together before the Lord ;

Chil. — For He is come to judge the earth.

Supt. — With righteousness shall He judge the world,

Chil. — And the people with equity.

VI.
Psalm c.

Supt. — O be joyful in the Lord, all ye lands ;

Chil. — Serve the Lord with gladness,

Supt. — And come before His presence with a song.

Chil. — Be ye sure that the Lord He is God ;

Supt. — It is He that hath made us, and not we ourselves;

Chil. — We are His people, and the sheep of His pasture.

Supt. — O go your way into His gates with thanksgiving,

Chil. — And into His courts with praise ;

Supt. — Be thankful unto Him, and speak good of His name,

Chil. — For the Lord is gracious ;

Supt. — His mercy is everlasting ;

Chil. — And His truth endureth from generation to generation.

VII.
From Psalms cxiii., cxv.

Supt. — Praise the Lord, O ye servants of His ;

Chil. — O praise the name of the Lord.

Supt. — Blessed be the name of the Lord,

Chil. — From this time forth for ever more.

Supt. — The Lord's name is praised, from the rising of the sun,

Chil. — Unto the going down of the same.

Supt. — The Lord is high above all nations,

Chil. — And His glory, above the heavens.

Supt. — Who is like unto the Lord our God, that hath His dwelling so high,

Chil. — And yet humbleth Himself to behold the things that are in heaven and earth?

Supt. — Ye that fear the Lord, put your trust in the Lord;

Chil. — For He is their help and their shield.

Supt. — He will bless them that fear the Lord, both small and great.

Chil. — Ye are the blessed of the Lord who made heaven and earth.

Supt. — The heaven, even the heavens, are the Lord's:

Chil. — But the earth hath He given to the children of men.

Supt. — The dead praise not the Lord,

Chil. — Neither any that go down into silence.

Supt. — But we will bless the Lord, from this time forth,

Chil. — And for ever more. Praise the Lord.

VIII.

Psalm cxxi.

Supt. — I will lift up mine eyes unto the hills,

Chil. — From whence cometh my help.

Supt. — My help cometh even from the Lord,

Chil. — Who hath made heaven and earth.

Supt. — He will not suffer thy foot to be moved ;

Chil. — And He that keepeth thee will not sleep.

Supt. — Behold, He that keepeth Israel,

Chil. — Shall neither slumber nor sleep.

Supt. — The Lord Himself is thy keeper ;

Chil. — The Lord is Thy defence upon thy right hand.

Supt. — So that the sun shall not burn thee by day,

Chil. — Neither the moon by night.

Supt. — The Lord shall preserve thee from all evil ;

Chil. — Yea, it is even He that shall keep thy soul.

Supt. — The Lord shall preserve thy going out and thy coming in,

Chil. — From this time forth, for ever more.

IX.

From Psalm cxxxvi.

Supt. — Oh give thanks unto the Lord ; for He is good :

Chil. — For His mercy endureth for ever.

Supt. — Oh, give thanks unto the God of gods :

Chil. — For His mercy endureth for ever.

Supt. — To Him who alone doeth great wonders ;

Chil. — For His mercy endureth for ever.

Supt. — To Him that by wisdom made the heavens :

Chil. — For His mercy endureth for ever.

Supt. — To Him that stretched out the earth above the waters :

Chil. — For His mercy endureth for ever.

Supt. — To Him that made great lights :

Chil. — For His mercy endureth for ever.

Supt. — The sun to rule by day ;

Chil. — For His mercy endureth for ever.

Supt. — The moon and stars to rule by night :

Chil. — For His mercy endureth for ever.

Supt. — Who remembered us in our low estate :

Chil. — For His mercy endureth for ever.

Supt. — Who giveth food to all flesh :

Chil. — For His mercy endureth for ever.

Supt. — Oh give thanks unto the God of heaven :

Chil. — For his mercy endureth for ever.

X.

From Psalm cxxxix.

Supt. — O Lord, Thou hast searched me out, and known me :

Chil. — Thou knowest my down-sitting and mine up-rising;

Supt. — Thou understandest my thoughts afar off.

Chil. — Thou art about my path, and about my bed,

Supt. — And art acquainted with all my ways.

Chil. — For lo, there is not a word in my tongue,

Supt. — But Thou, O Lord, knowest it altogether.

Chil. — Thou hast beset me behind and before,

Supt. — And laid Thine hand upon me.

Chil. — Such knowledge is too wonderful for me :

Supt. — It is high, I can not attain unto it.

Chil. — Whither shall I go from Thy spirit?

Supt. — Or whither shall I flee from Thy presence ?

Chil. — If I ascend up into Heaven, Thou art there ;

Supt. — If I make my bed in the grave, behold, Thou art there.

Chil. — If I take the wings of the morning,

Supt. — And dwell in the uttermost parts of the sea ;

Chil. — Even there also shall Thy hand lead me,

Supt. — And Thy right hand shall hold me.

Chil. — If I say, surely the darkness shall cover me ;

Supt. — Then shall the night be turned to day,

Chil. — Yea, the darkness is no darkness with Thee,

Supt. — But the night is as clear as the day ;

Chil. — The darkness and light to Thee are both alike.

Supt. — How precious are Thy thoughts unto me, O God !

Chil. — How great is the sum of them !

Supt. — If I should count them, they are more in number than the sand :

Chil. — When I awake, I am still with Thee.

Supt. — Search me, O God, and know my heart :

Chil. — Try me, and know my thoughts :

Supt. — And see if there be any wicked way in me,

Chil. — And lead me in the way everlasting.

XI.

From Psalm cxlvii.

Supt. — Praise ye the Lord :

Chil. — For it is good to sing praises unto our God ;

Supt. — For it is pleasant ;

Chil. — And praise is comely.

Supt. — He healeth the broken in heart,

Chil. — And bindeth up their wounds.

Supt. — He telleth the number of the stars;

Chil. — He calleth them all by their names.

Supt. — Sing unto the Lord with thanksgiving;

Chil. — Sing praises upon the harp unto our God :

Supt. — Who covereth the heaven with clouds,

Chil. — Who prepareth rain for the earth,

Supt. — Who maketh grass to grow upon the mountains.

Chil. — He giveth to the beast his food,

Supt. — And to the young ravens which cry.

Chil. — He giveth snow like wool :

Supt. — He scattereth the hoar frost like ashes.

Chil. — He casteth forth His ice like morsels :

Supt. — Who can stand before His cold ?

Chil. — He sendeth out His word and melteth them :

Supt. — He causeth the wind to blow, and the waters flow.

Chil. — He hath not dealt so with any nation :

Supt. — And as for His judgments, they have not known them.

Chil. — Praise ye the Lord.

XII.

Psalm cl.

Supt. — O Praise God in His sanctuary :

Chil. — Praise Him in the firmament of His power.

Supt. — Praise Him for His mighty acts :

Chil. — Praise Him according to His excellent greatness.

Supt. — Praise Him with the sound of the trumpet ;

Chil. — Praise Him upon the lute and the harp:

Supt. — Praise Him in the cymbals and dances :

Chil. — Praise Him upon the strings and pipe:

Supt. — Praise Him upon the well-tuned cymbals :

Chil. — Praise Him upon the loud cymbals.

Supt. — Let every thing that hath breath praise the Lord.

Chil. — Praise ye the Lord.

BEATITUDES.

Supt. — Blessed are the poor in spirit :

Chil. — For theirs is the kingdom of heaven.

Supt. — Blessed are they that mourn :

Chil. — For they shall be comforted.

Supt. — Blessed are the meek :

Chil. — For they shall inherit the earth.

Supt. — Blessed are they which do hunger and thirst after righteousness :

Chil. — For they shall be filled.

Supt. — Blessed are the merciful :

Chil. — For they shall obtain mercy.

Supt. — Blessed are the pure in heart :

Chil. — For they shall see God.

Supt. — Blessed are the peacemakers :

Chil. — For they shall be called the children of God.

Supt.—Blessed are they which are persecuted for righteousness' sake :

Chil.—For theirs is the kingdom of heaven.

Supt. — Come unto me all ye that labor and are heavy laden,

Chil. — And I will give you rest.

Supt. — Take my yoke upon you, and learn of me ;

Chil. — For I am meek and lowly in heart :

Supt. — And ye shall find rest unto your souls,

Chil.—For my yoke is easy, and my burden is light.

THE COMMANDMENTS.

Supt. — He that hath my commandments, and keepeth them, he it is that loveth me :

Chil. — And he that loveth me shall be loved of my Father,

Supt. — And I will love him, and will manifest myself to him.

Chil. — If ye love me, keep my commandments.

Supt. — And God spake all these words ;

Chil. — Thou shalt have no other gods before me.

Supt. — Thou shalt not make unto thee any graven image, or any likeness of any thing that is in heaven above, or earth beneath, or that is in the waters under the earth:

Chil. — Thou shalt not bow down thyself to them nor serve them.

Supt. — Thou shalt not take the name of the Lord thy God in vain.

Chil. — Remember the Sabbath day to keep it holy.

Supt. — Honor thy father and thy mother.

Chil. — Thou shalt not kill.

Supt. — Thou shalt not commit adultery.

Chil. — Thou shalt not steal.

Supt. — Thou shalt not bear false witness.

Chil. — Thou shalt not covet.

Supt. — O Lord, put these Thy laws into our minds,

Chil. — And write them in our hearts.

Supt. — And Thou shalt love us, and wilt come unto us,

Chil. — And make Thy abode with us.

ADDITIONAL PRAYERS.

TO BE USED AT THE OPENING OF THE SCHOOL.

———◆●◆———

I.

OUR Father, we pray Thee to be with us — and bless us this day.—Dangers are round us by day and by night.—Save us, O God, from all that can wound the body, or hurt the soul.—Our lives are in Thy hand, — and to Thee do we look for help in every time of need.

Lord, teach us to keep Thee ever in our thought, — that we may fall into no evil way. —When we go out, and when we come in ; — when alone, and when we are with others, — may we bear in mind that Thou art with us, — and that Thou knowest all we think, and say, and do.

We pray that we may be brought up in Thy love.—Grant us, O Lord, strength to serve Thee always.—Help us day by day to amend our ways, — that we may grow in grace, — and learn more and more — how we may walk so as to please Thee.

Give us only such things as we need.— And that Thou wilt hear and answer our prayers,—may we ask for the right things.— We pray Thee to lead us safely through this life, — and to bring us to the end of our days in peace. — Forgive all our sins, — our evil thoughts, and words and deeds, — through Jesus Christ our Lord. *Amen.*

II.

OUR Father who art in heaven: — Thou art the source of all our hopes,—both in this world — and in that which is to come :— To Thee do we owe life, and health, and all things.

Thou hast cared for us in infancy:—Be Thou our guide in youth.—Watch over us in all the years to come.—Thou hast healed us when we were sick.—Thou hast raised us up when we have been brought low.—Day after day Thou hast been with us, — and comforts are round us on every side.

O Lord, we bless Thy name for what is past.—May the thought of Thy goodness lead us to repent of all our sins.—May we walk in Thy will in the time to come. — Help us this day to shun all that is wrong. —Grant, that as we love life, — and wish to see good days, — we may keep our tongues from evil, — and our lips from guile.—Give us, we pray Thee, right minds, that we

may see Thy truth.—And grant us meek
hearts — that we may enter into Thy kingdom.—And when it shall please Thee to call
us from this world, — may we give our souls
with trust and hope into Thy hands.—We
ask it through Christ.—*Amen.*

III.

LORD of all power and grace, — who alone
art holy, just and true :—We are filled
with grief and shame—when we think of all
our sins against Thee.—Well may we put our
hands upon our mouths — and our faces in
the dust, — for we choose the dark ways of
sin, — rather than the light of Thy truth.

But O, our Father, we bless Thy name that
Thou hast given us hope.—Thou hast said if
we turn from our evil ways and repent, —
Thou wilt forgive the wrong we do.—We
pray Thee now to take us into Thy favor, —
that we may dwell in that kingdom — which
is in every soul — that is filled with Thy
truth and love.

We thank Thee O God, for the gift of Thy
Son.—Thou didst send him into the world to
make known Thy ways.—May we aim to be
like him—to have his spirit—to be ready like
him at all times, — to do and to bear for the
sake of Thy truth.—Make our hearts a fit
abode for Thy blessed spirit.—Guard us from
all that is wrong in Thy sight.—And make
us Thine in word and deed — through Jesus
Christ our Lord. *Amen.*

IV.

THY dear Son, O God, when on earth—took up little children in his arms and blessed them.—Fold us, Father, in Thine arms, and bless us also.—Fill our hearts, we pray Thee, with love, — and open our lips with praise.— Every good thing we have comes from Thee. —Thou art helping us by day and by night— and giving us food, and raiment and health.— We bless Thee for these Thy gifts.—But more than all, we bless Thee for the great love of Christ, — for the means of grace, — and for the hope of the life to come.—O Lord, we pray Thee to look in much mercy upon this School.—Give those who teach a deep sense of the great work they have to do.—Grant them every gift they need.—May they have joy in training up the young—in the way they should go,—that when they are old, they may not depart from it.

And bless these Children in their studies.— May they be quick to learn.—May they keep the lessons they are taught.—May they obey their Parents and Teachers,—and be kind to each other.—And as they grow in grace,— may they also grow in wisdom,—and in favor with God and man.

O Lord, be with us all, Teachers and Children,—at all times and in all places.— Graft in our hearts the love of Thy name.— Increase in us true religion.—Build us up in Thy most holy faith,—and keep us ever in the right way.—We ask it through Jesus Christ our Lord. *Amen.*

V.

TO Thee, O God, we owe life,—and health and all things.—No tongue can tell, no thought can sound the depths of Thy love.—When we lie down, it is under the shadow of Thy wings.—When we rise up, Thy hand leads us,—and Thy right hand upholds us.—In Thee we live and move and have our being.—Make us to feel, O God, that we are never alone.—Thine eye is ever fixed upon us.—Thou art with us in every good word and work.—O let not our hearts be so hard,—our minds so dark,—and our lives so false,—that we lose sight of this truth.—When the tempter .calls—may the thought that Thou, God, seest us,—keep us in the right way.—May we feel that to Thine eye our souls are never closed.

May we live this day, as they should live,— who know not what a day may bring forth.— May it be thine, and each event which it brings,—lead us nearer to Thee.—Give us grace for the work Thou wouldst have us do. —Save us from all sin,—and make us clean in heart,—and pure in mind.—Teach us to forgive those who wrong us,—as we are forgiven by Thee.—And bring us all at last—to that place of rest and peace—which Thou hast prepared for us.—And if these our prayers come from our hearts,—hear and answer them,—through Jesus Christ our Lord. *Amen.*

VI.

MOST gracious God, Thou hast kept us through the night,—Thou hast given us sweet sleep,—and hast brought us here in peace.—We give Thee most hearty thanks, —and praise Thee for these, and for all Thy gifts.—Take away all our sins,—and make our lives pure,—that we may be more worthy to come into Thy sight.

Thou wilt hear the prayers of those whose hearts are set to do Thy will.—We come to Thee now,—and ask Thee to make Thy face to shine upon us.—We have not heard Thy voice.—We have strayed from Thy ways like lost sheep.—O call us back to Thy fold, we pray Thee.—Make us to lie down in green pastures.—Lead us beside the still waters.— And let not the things of this world—come between our souls and Thee.—We can not thank Thee as we ought,—for all Thou hast done for us.—With our very first breath we drank in Thy love.—And every step that we take in life,—every morning and every night, —brings, us fresh proofs of Thy care.—May these truths dwell in our minds,—that we may do Thy will on earth—as it is done in heaven.—And let not our words dwell only on our lips,—but may we do as we say,—and

while we ask Thine aid,—may we seek to do
Thy will.—And to Thee, the God of our
lives,—the source of all good,—we will give
the praise—through Jesus Christ our Lord.
Amen.

VII.

FATHER in Heaven, Thou hast sent us
another Sabbath-day,—May we find the
rest which it gives.—Grant that our souls
may be fed with bread from Heaven.—May
each hour show that our hearts are right,—
and that our feet are in the way of life.—We
pray Thee to be with us and to bless us,—
now and to the end of our days.—Without
Thee we can do nothing.—With Thee nothing
can make us afraid.—For every step that we
take,—for every breath that we breathe,—
strength comes from Thee.—Thy smile is
life,—and Thy love is better than life.

When we forget Thee,—send down the
light of Thy truth upon our path.—May we
take heed when we think we stand,—lest we
fall.—And O, may we not think our own
strength is all we need.—May we feel that
Thou art ever nigh to guide and to guard
us,—and wilt do more for us than we can
ask or think.

Thy grace, O God, is a free gift.—We can
do Thee no good.—There is nothing we can
give Thee.—And yet Thou dost care for us.
—What shall we say unto Thee?—What

shall we bring Thee for all Thy love ?—We can only pray that we may have a deep sense of Thy goodness,—and that we may have Thee in all our thoughts.

And as the words of prayer cease from our lips,—may the life of prayer dwell in our hearts.—Be Thou with us now and ever more.—We ask it through Jesus Christ our Lord. *Amen.*

VIII.

OUR Father, the preserver of our lives,— and the giver of every good gift.—We pray Thee to be with us in every scene of life.—Give us strength to bear all the sickness and pains that may come upon us.—And grant us grace to thank Thee—for all the joys Thou shalt send us.

Teach us to know our duty in all things.— May we do to others as we would have them do to us.—May we wrong no one in word or deed.—May we be just and true in all things. —May we bear no evil thought in our hearts. —May we guard our hands that they do no wrong,—and our tongues that they speak no guile.—And may we not long for the goods of another,—but may we be content with our own.

We pray Thee, O Lord, to bless our School.—Here may we learn to walk in the light.—May we take Thy truth, here taught us, into our hearts,—and ever hold fast that

which is good.—And let it be our aim to
build up Thy cause in the world.—Lead us in
the right way,—that we may run into no
folly.—And may we be so trained to serve
Thee here,—that we may not have lived in
vain.—And when Thou shalt have done with
us here,—take us to dwell with Thee in
Heaven.—We ask it through Christ. *Amen.*

IX.

FATHER in Heaven, we come to ask Thy
blessing.—We pray that we may love
and trust Thee more—and serve Thee better.
And to this end grant us a true sense of
Thy presence.—May we find peace in the
thought,—that Thou art not far from any one
of us.—And thus may this day, and every
day, be Thy day,—and our bodies and souls,
—with all their powers, be Thine for ever.

Fix in us Thy faith, and fear, and love.—
Grant us light to know,—and strength to do
Thy will.—When we err, have pity on us.—
When we stray from the right way, bring us
back.—And O, give us a clear view of sin,—
and a deep sense of our guilt, when we yield
to sin.—Teach us to watch our hearts,—that
we may check our tongues,—and rule our
tempers.—May our words and works be such
that we shall be Thine,—and every good
thing we ask shall be ours.—Almighty God,
since Thou hast formed us for Thyself,—since
we have minds to see,—and hearts to feel

how good Thou art,—give us the will to
serve Thee now and always.—We ask it in
the name of Thy dear Son, our Lord. *Amen.*

X.

THOU alone, O God, art great and good.—
Thou alone art holy.—Thou sittest in the
heaven of heavens.—Before Thee the angels
veil their faces,—and the heavens are not
clean in Thy sight.—We are weak, and need
Thy gracious arm to lean upon.—We are sinful, and our only help is in Thee.

Often when we would seek Thy face,—our
praises are cold and dead,—and we come to
Thee with our lips,—when our hearts are far
from Thee.—The vain shows of the world
charm us,—and lead our feet in the ways of
sin.—O Lord, open Thou our eyes,—that we
may see not only where we are,—but where
we ought to be.—We pray Thee to help us
this day.—Guard both our bodies and our
souls,—from all that can do them harm.—
Help us to feel that we are not our own, but
Thine.—Thy dear Son died to save us from
sin.—He gave his life on the cross,—that we
might be free :—that he might win us by his
love,—to give our lives to Thee.

Grant, Lord, that we may have a clear
sense—of what Christ has done for us.—
Teach us to look to him,—to see his holy life,
—and to live as he did.—May we show how
much we love Thee,—by walking in his ways.
—We ask it in the name of Jesus. *Amen.*

RECOVERY FROM SICKNESS.

WE thank Thee, O God, for all things.—
We thank Thee for life and health.—
We bless Thee that Thou hast given new
strength to our friend who was sick —*He*
was brought low, and Thou didst help *him*.
—*He* was on the verge of the grave,—and
Thou didst give *him* back to us.—We pray
for *him*.—We pray that the life which Thou
hast spared—may be given with all its
powers to Thee.—We pray for ourselves.—
May we lay up these warnings in our hearts.
—In hours of joy,—let us not lose sight of
the days that are gone.—And when the dark
hour shall come for us,—may we be still, and
know that Thou art God.

And as we look back on the past,—may
we have strength from Thee for the time to
come.—Warned that our days on earth are
few,—and are soon gone,—may our love be
pure in Thy sight.—Let us not lay up
treasures on earth,—where all that is fair
and bright, fades and dies.—But may we lay
up stores of truth and love,—which death
can never reach.—May we shun all that is
wrong,—and cleave to that which is good.—
Do Thou reign, O God, in our hearts.—Be
Thou loved with all our strength,—and give
us the joy of true minds.—Fill us with Thy
Spirit,—that we may grow more and more
like Thee,—till we come to dwell with
Thee and Thy Son,—in the world that

shall have no end.—Hear and answer our prayer—through Jesus Christ our Lord. Amen.

ON ENTERING CHURCH.

GOD of love and truth,—who dost ever help those who come to Thee :—Grant that the words I shall hear this day may give me strength,—and lead me in the way of life, and keep me in Thy love.—Help me to love Thee and do Thy will,—that my whole life may show forth Thy praise.—Let the words of my mouth,—and the thoughts of my heart,—be pure in Thy sight,—O Lord, my strength, and my Redeemer.

FOR GOD'S BLESSING ON THE INSTRUCTION OF HIS WORD.

FATHER in Heaven, Thy word is true.— It leads the soul in the way of life.—It makes wise the simple,—gives sight to the blind,—and saves from the sin that is in the world—all who truly believe.—And as we are prone to let go the things which make our peace,—and as Thou wilt help those who come to Thee to learn Thy truth,—we pray Thee to cause the light of Thy word to shine in our minds,—and give us a heart free from all pride—and trust in our own strength,—that we may hear that word, and know what it means,—that our lives may be
5*

such as shall please Thee.—We pray Thee to turn all those who still stray from Thy truth, —that they may serve Thee as dear children— all the days of their life.—We ask it through Jesus Christ our Lord. *Amen.*

AN EVENING PRAYER.

FATHER in Heaven, Thou art light,—and in Thee is no darkness at all.—Thou makest the darkness, and it is night.—And yet to Thee the night is as the day.—Thou art with us always.—Thine eye, which is never closed,—sees us while we sleep.—Thou hast made the day for toil,—and the night for rest.—And now that the day which Thou hast given us is done,—and the shades of night fall on our way,—grant that our bodies may rest in peace,—that they may have new strength for the work they must do.—Let us go to our rest leaning on Thine arm.—May the sense of Thy presence give peace to our sleep.—And if it be Thy will to send us another day,—may we spend its hours—as we shall wish we had,—when we come to look back.

We give ourselves with full trust to Thy care,—not only for this night,—but at all times.—Gather us, O God, under the wings of Thy care always,—and when the last night shall come,—may we fall asleep in Jesus,—and awake in that world,—where we shall walk forever in the light of Thy love ;

—for there shall be no night there.—We ask it through Jesus Christ our Lord. *Amen.*

PRAYER IN TIME OF GREAT TROUBLE.

OUR Father who art in Heaven,—we would call to Thee in our trouble ;—for in Thee is all our trust.—Thou who hast formed our eyes, canst see us.—Thou who hast made our ears, canst hear us.—Thou who hast given us hearts, canst feel for us.—We will carry our cares only to Thee.—We will open our hearts, and show Thee the grief that is too heavy for us to bear. For we know, O our Father, that Thou wilt lift from our souls that which we are too weak to remove. Hear the prayers of Thy children, and answer them in Thy great love. We ask it through Christ our Saviour. *Amen.*

ADDITIONAL PRAYERS,

TO BE USED AT THE CLOSE OF THE SCHOOL.

I.

O LORD, from whom all good gifts do come ; grant that we may use them to our profit, and to Thy praise.

Let Thy blessing go with the lessons which we have this day learned. Teach us to be glad in Thy truth, that we may love Thee with all our hearts. May it be our chief joy to worship Thee, and to give Thee thanks. May we honor Thy holy name and word, and serve Thee to the end of our days. Blot out all our sins, and be with us for ever. Hear our prayer, and grant us all we need, through Jesus Christ our Lord. *Amen.*

To God, the only wise, be glory through Jesus Christ, for ever. *Amen.*

II.

WE bless Thee, O God, for the light of Thy word. May we in such wise hear, read, and learn it, that we may be saved from the sin that is in the world. And may we find, and ever hold fast the hope of the life to come.

May all who have the gospel of Thy dear Son, live in its light and walk in its truth. Pardon all our sins. Guard us by night and by day. Save us from all that can do us harm. Unite us in the bonds of love. Build us up in Thy faith. In this faith would we live and die. And in its joy would we go to dwell with Thee in Heaven. *Amen.*

To God, the only wise, be glory now and ever more. *Amen.* '

III.

WE thank Thee, Father, that Thou hast given us Thy word, and that we are taught Thy truth. May we learn to love that truth. May it be so fixed in our minds, that with the faith of Christ on our lips, and in our hearts, we may know and do Thy will. So shall our tongues praise Thee with songs of joy, and our hearts shall love Thee more than words can tell.

Go with us to our homes. Be with us when we shall go out into the world, to shield us from all harm. Blot out all our sins that we may be Thine in will and deed. We ask it through Thy Son, our Saviour. *Amen.*

The grace of our Lord Jesus Christ, keep you in the truth and love of God, world without end. *Amen.*

IV.

WE pray Thee, O Lord, that we may read Thy will in all Thy works. May the light of the day call us to Thy praise. May the shades of night tell us of Thy care. With glad hearts may we joy in Thy work. May we hold time as Thy gift, and use it well. May the love we bear our friends lead us to Thee, for Thou, O God, art love. May the world in which we live, teach us of a world more bright to come. Take away all our past sins, and may we be pure in heart. Go with us from Thy house, and be with us now and ever more. *Amen.*

The grace of our Lord Jesus Christ, and the love of God, and the communion of the Holy Spirit, be with us all ever more. *Amen.*

V.

O LORD, the hope of those who put their trust in Thee: Go with us from this Thy house. Grant that the lessons we have learned this day, may be so fixed in our minds, that they may bring forth fruit in our lives, to the praise of Thy name.

And while we bless Thee with our tongues, may we much more bless Thee in our hearts and lives. Let both our words and works show forth Thy praise.

Blot out all our sins, our vain thoughts and words and deeds. And grant us grace for the time to come. We ask it in the name of Jesus. *Amen.*

Peace be with you, and love, with faith, from God the Father, and the Lord Jesus Christ. *Amen.*

VI.

THOU, Father, art nigh to those who call on Thee in truth. Thou wilt hear the prayer of those who love Thee, and save them. We bow before Thy throne, O God, and though we see Thee not with the eye, nor hear Thee with the ear, we are taught by Thy word and works, that Thou art, and that Thou art not far from any one of us.

And now, that Thy name is on our lips, write Thy laws in our hearts, that we may have length of days, and years of life and peace. And when these days and years shall end, take us to dwell with Thee in Heaven. We ask it through Christ. *Amen.*

The grace of our Lord Jesus Christ be with you all. *Amen.*

VII.

GOD of love and truth, may we know that Thou art our Father, and feel that we are Thy children. Teach us what Thou wouldst have us do, that we may do it with our might. And as we are poor and weak, may we find our strength in Thee. May the words we have heard this day bring us

nigh to Thee, and make us love Thee more.
Forgive all our sins, our idle thoughts,
and words and deeds. And since Thou art
Lord of heaven and earth, take us to Thyself when Thou shalt call us hence. We ask
it in the name of him who died that we
might live. *Amen.*

Grace be with you all. *Amen.*

VIII.

WE would seek Thy face, O God, for they
that seek Thee early shall find Thee.
May it be good for us to be here, that we
may be taught Thy word, and walk in Thy
paths.

We thank Thee that we can here learn the
truth as it is in Jesus. Let its light shine
in our hearts, so that we may know Thee
as Thou art.

We pray Thee, O Lord, to bless our
School. May those who teach be taught of
Thee, and those who learn be led in the
right way. Go with us when we shall go
hence. And guard, and guide and bless us,
now and ever more, through Jesus Christ
our Lord. *Amen.*

The Lord of peace go with you, and give
you peace now and always. *Amen.*

IX.

THOU art, O God, the first and the last,
and there is no God but Thee. No eye
hath seen Thee, nor can see Thee. But as

we see Thee in Thy works, and learn of Thee in Thy word, may the great truth that Thou art, be so fixed in our hearts, that we may live as though we saw, and were seen by Thee. May we show that we love Thee whom we have not seen, by our love for those whom we do see.

And at the last, when we shall see as we are seen, and know as we are known, may we see, and know and love Thee, through Christ our Lord. *Amen*

Peace be with you, and love, with faith, from God the Father, and the Lord Jesus Christ. *Amen.*

X.

THOU art, O God, a God of love. Make Thy love to dwell in our hearts, that we may show it in our lives, in kind words and deeds, which we may do at all times.

May we trust in Thee, that when we come here in Thy name, Thou wilt be with us and bless us, and that what we ask in faith, Thou wilt give us. And to Thy name, through him, who is the way, the truth and the life, be praise now and ever more. *Amen.*

The grace of the Lord Jesus Christ, and the love of God, and the communion of the Holy Ghost, be with you all. *Amen.*

6

CHRISTMAS.

COLLECT.

SOURCE of light and truth, Who didst send Thy Son, Jesus Christ, into the world, that the world through him might be saved : Grant that the light of his truth may shine into our hearts, and guide our steps, and lead us to Thee. So shall we be born of God, Thy children in very deed and Truth. We ask it in the name of Thy Son our Saviour. *Amen.*

SCRIPTURE LESSON.

And there were in the same country, shep herds abiding in the field, keeping watch over their flocks by night.

And lo ! the angel of the Lord came upon them, and the glory of the Lord shone round about them, and they were sore afraid.

And the angel said unto them : fear not, for behold, I bring you good tidings of great joy which shall be to all people.

For unto you is born this day in the city of David, a Saviour, who is Christ the Lord.

And this shall be a sign unto you ; ye shall find the babe wrapped in swaddling clothes, lying in a manger.

And suddenly there was with the angel a multitude of the heavenly host praising God, and saying :

Glory be to God in the highest, and on earth peace, good will to men.

PSALM.

From xcvi Psalm.

Supt.—O sing unto the Lord a new song:

Chil.—Sing unto the Lord, all the earth.

Supt.—Sing unto the Lord, bless His name ;

Chil.—Show forth His salvation from day to day.

Supt.—For the Lord is great, and greatly to be praised:

Chil.—He is to be feared above all gods.

Supt.—Honor and majesty are before Him :

Chil.—Strength and beauty are in His sanctuary.

Supt.—Give unto the Lord, O ye kindreds of the people,

Chil.—Give unto the Lord glory and strength.

Supt.—Give unto the Lord the glory due unto His name :

Chil.—Bring an offering, and come into His courts.

Supt.—O worship the Lord in the beauty of holiness :

Chil.—Fear before Him all the earth.

Supt.—Let the heavens rejoice, and let the earth be glad ;

Chil.—Let the sea roar, and the fulness thereof.

Supt.—Let the field be joyful, and all that therein is :

Chil.—Then shall all the trees of the wood rejoice before the Lord :

Supt.—For He cometh, for He cometh to judge the earth:

Chil.—He shall judge the world with righteousness,

Supt.—And the people with His truth.

PRAYER.

WE bless Thee, our Father, for the gift of Thy dear Son. For all He did and suffered, we bring Thee this day, the gift of joy and praise. We bless Thee for his words of truth. We thank Thee for his firm faith and for his great love. We praise Thee for his power over sin and death, and for his resurrection.

O may we never prove false to the great truths for which Christ gave his body to be broken, and his blood to be poured out on the cross. May the words that we say with our lips come warm from our hearts. May the works that we do with our hands be done with no eye to the praise of men. So shall we grow up in the likeness of the Lord Jesus, and be filled with Thy truth. So shall we know what a great thing it is to live, and have strength for the work that is given us to do.

And grant, Father, that our blessed Saviour who came into the world to do Thy will, may rule in every heart. May every eye see him, and every tongue confess him to be the Lord, to the glory of Thee the Father, whom we worship one God, through Jesus Christ our Lord, now and ever more. *Amen.*

FOR THE NEW YEAR.

COLLECT.

FATHER in Heaven, Thou who art, and wast, and art to come,—in Thee we live, and move, and have our being. At the dawn of *a New Year we come to seek Thy blessing. And now, while we feel that Thou art with us we give ourselves anew to Thy service. With one mind and heart we pause at this time, and pray for light. Send down Thy Spirit to write upon our hearts what Thou wouldst have us do. We ask it in the name of Jesus Christ. *Amen.*

PSALM.
From Psalm cii.

Supt.—My days are like a shadow that declineth ;

Chil.—And I am withered like grass.

Supt.—But Thou, O Lord, shalt endure for ever ;

Chil.—And Thy remembrance to all generations.

Supt.—O my God, take me not away in the midst of my days :

Chil.—As for Thy years, they endure throughout all generations.

Supt.—Thou Lord, in the beginning hast laid the foundation of the earth,

Chil.—And the heavens are the work of Thy hands.

Supt. They shall perish, but Thou shalt endure ;

C*

Chil.—They all shall wax old as a garment.

Supt.—And as a vesture shalt Thou change them, and they shall be changed ;

Chil.—But Thou art the same, and Thy years shall have no end.

PRAYER.

FATHER in Heaven, may the year now come, prove to us a new year indeed. May it bring new and pure thoughts to our minds. May we aim to be better, and live nearer to Thee than we have in the past. Happy, blessed will it be for us if the new year shall lead us into a diviner life.

It may bring us trials and sorrows, and take from us health and friends. Still, we shall be happy if through Thy grace we use it well. It may strip us of the joys we hold most dear, yet we shall be rich indeed if it make us wise and good, if we shall learn to trust Thee more, and love Thee better.

We may not live to see the dawn of another year. Long ere this shall end we may die. But, O Thou, in whose hands are life and death, living or dying, may we be found doing Thy work. Teach us to live wisely and well, and to grow in truth and love in every year and day to come.

And when time shall be no more, bring us, we pray Thee, to dwell with Thee in Thy house not made with hands. And Thee will we praise, world without end through Jesus Christ our Lord. *Amen.*

EASTER.

COLLECT.

FATHER in Heaven, who by Thy Son hast burst the bars of death, and opened to our souls the gates of light and life: Grant that as we have this hope we may be pure even as he is pure : That we may always serve Thee with pure hearts and clean hands : And that through all the changes of this world our hearts may surely there be fixed where true joys are to be found. We ask it through Jesus Christ our Lord. *Amen.*

SCRIPTURE LESSON.

Luke xxiv. 1–6.

Upon the first day of the week, very early in the morning, they came unto the sepulchre, bringing the spices which they had prepared, and certain others with them.

And they found the stone rolled away from the sepulchre.

And they entered in, and found not the body of the Lord Jesus.

And it came to pass, as they were much perplexed thereabout, behold, two men stood by them in shining garments.

And as they were afraid, and bowed down their faces to the earth, they said unto them, Why seek ye the living among the dead ?

He is not here, but is risen.

PSALM.

From Psalms xxiv., xlvii.

Supt.—Lift up your heads, O ye gates ;

Chil.—And be ye lifted up, ye everlasting doors ;

Supt.—And the King of glory shall come in.

Chil.—Who is the King of glory ?

Supt.—It is the Lord strong and mighty,

Chil.—Even the Lord mighty in battle.

Supt.—Lift-up your heads, O ye gates ;

Chil.—And be ye lifted up, ye everlasting doors ;

Supt.—And the King of glory shall come in.

Chil.—Who is the King of glory ?

Supt.—Even the Lord of hosts, He is the King of glory.

Chil.—Clap your hands together, all ye people :

Supt.—O sing unto God with the voice of melody. .

Chil.—God is gone up with a shout,

Supt.—And the Lord with the sound of a trumpet.

Chil.—O sing praises, sing praises unto our God ;

Supt.—O sing praises, sing praises unto our King,   .

Chil.—For God is the King of all the earth ;

Supt.—Sing ye praises with understanding.

Chil.—God sitteth upon the throne of His holiness.

PRAYER.

WE adore Thee, O God. Thou hast made heaven and earth. All that we see is full of Thy great glory.

We bless Thee that Thou didst send Thy Son into the world, that the world through him might be saved. We bless Thee that he died and was buried. Thou didst raise him from the dead. Through Thy power he came forth from the grave. The gates of death were thrown open, and he came forth from the place of the dead, and trod the earth with his holy feet. And his voice was heard to speak peace to men.

Open our eyes, O God, to see the truth of Thy word. May we feel the power of his resurrection. We praise Thee for the light, and hope and joy that were in Christ. We know the life that was in him was the life and power of God. And as we have seen him, we have seen Thee, the Father. And we know Thou art the Father, and we are Thy children.

God Most High, who hast given Thy Son to die for our sins, and raised him from the dead that we might have hope, grant us so to put away every evil thought and deed, that we may always serve Thee with clean hearts. Teach the whole world of him who died that we might live. May the love that was in him dwell in all hearts. And to Thee, through Jesus Christ our Lord, shall be the praise, now and ever more. *Amen.*

SPECIAL SERVICE.

To be used in case of the Dangerous Illness of a Member of the School.

----- •♦• -----

INTRODUCTORY SENTENCES.

Father in Heaven; all things that Thou hast made wait upon Thee, that Thou mayest give them their meat in due season.

When Thou givest it them, they gather it, and when Thou openest Thine hand, they are filled with good.

When Thou sendest forth Thy spirit, they are created: When Thou hidest Thy face, they are troubled: When Thou takest away their breath, they die, and are turned again to their dust.

SCRIPTURE LESSON.

Matthew xxvi. 36.

Then cometh Jesus with them unto a place called Gethsemane, and saith unto the disciples, Sit ye here, while I go and pray yonder.

And he took with him Peter and the two

sons of Zebedee, and began to be sorrowful and very heavy.

Then saith he unto them, my soul is exceeding sorrowful, even unto death: tarry ye here, and watch with me.

And he went a little further, and fell on his face, and prayed, saying, O, my Father, if it be possible, let this cup pass from me : nevertheless, not as I will, but as Thou wilt.

PSALM.

Psalm xxiii.

Supt.—The Lord is my shepherd ;

Chil.—I shall not want.

Supt.—He maketh me to lie down in green pastures ;

Chil.—He leadeth me beside the still waters.

Supt.—He restoreth my soul :

Chil.—He leadeth me in the paths of righteousness for His name's sake.

Supt.—Yea, though I walk through the valley of the shadow of death,

Chil.—I will fear no evil :

Supt.—For Thou art with me ;

Chil.—Thy rod and Thy staff they comfort me.

Supt.—Thou preparest a table before me in the presence of mine enemies :

Chil.—Thou anointest my head with oil ; my cup runneth over.

Supt.—Surely goodness and mercy shall follow me all the days of my life :

Chil.—And I will dwell in the house of the Lord for ever.

[For a Child.]

PRAYER.

O LORD, the hope of all who put their trust in Thee, may we see Thy ruling hand in all things. May we feel it is better to have Thy will done than our own. May we bear with meek hearts what it may please Thee to send us. And when Thy hand is laid upon us, may our hearts be still, and know that it is God.

Hear, O Lord, the prayers we offer for Thy child, who is kept from this place by sickness. May it please Thee to look upon *him*, and give *him* Thy grace as *he* shall need. Spare the fond hopes bound up in *his* life, and let this bitter cup pass from us. But Thy will, O God, not ours be done.

If it shall please Thee to remove *his* pains, and bring *him* back to health and strength, may *he* live to Thy praise.

But if it shall be Thy will that this sickness shall be unto death, fit *him* for Thy courts above. Grant that *he* may leave this world in peace, and be ready for that which is so much better. Take *him* to that place of rest, where the tears shall be wiped from all eyes; where there shall be no more death, where *he* shall see the joy of Thy face, and live in the light of Thy love.

And grant, O God, that whether we live,

we may live unto Thee, or whether we die,
we may die unto Thee : so that living or
dying, we may be Thine. O Lord, in Thee
have we put our trust, let us never be cast
down. We ask it in the name of thy Son,
our Saviour. *Amen.*

[For a Teacher, or an Older Scholar.]

PRAYER.

FATHER of mercies, in Thee alone are
hope and peace. Thou knowest all our
wants, and wilt grant us such things as we
need. Thou hearest our prayers for that
dear one of our number, now kept from this
place by sickness. Thou knowest how much
we wish *he* may not die. O bless, we pray
Thee, the means used to bring *him* back to
health. O spare *him* that *he* may have new
strength. Turn our grief into joy. Let Thy
servant live and bless Thy name.

Let not our will, O God, but Thine be
done. Be this the prayer of our hearts, as
well as of our lips. May we trust in Thee,
and yield to Thee in all things. And above
all, may *he* who is sick have firm faith in
Thee. Fill *his* heart with a sense of Thy
great love. May thoughts of Thee and
heaven lift *his* soul above the things of time.

And let not these voices of life and death
fall on our ears alone. Let them be heard in
our hearts. May they teach us to trust Thee
at all times. And so shall we not fear to

7

part with our friends, when Thou shalt call them away.

And grant, O God, that we may have that faith in Thy dear Son, which takes the sting from death, and from the grave its fear.

Father in Heaven be with us. Still every doubt, hush every sigh, fill every heart with peace. And whether our friends stay with us, or go to dwell with Thee, may our faith in Thee be firm and sure. And Thee will we praise, through Jesus Christ, now and in the world to come. *Amen.*

SPECIAL SERVICE.

To be used in case of the Death of a Member of the School.

———◆●◆———

[For a child.]

INTRODUCTORY SENTENCES.

We brought nothing into this world, and it is very certain that we can carry nothing out. The Lord gave, and the Lord hath taken away; blessed be the name of the Lord.

And David said, while the child was yet alive, I fasted and wept: for I said, who can tell whether God will be gracious to me, that the child may live?

But now he is dead, wherefore should I fast? Can I bring him back again? I shall go to him, but he shall not return to me.

Is it well with the child? It is well.

And they shall be mine, saith the Lord of hosts, in the day when I make up my jewels.

———

[For a Teacher, or an older Scholar.]

INTRODUCTORY SENTENCES.

I am the resurrection and the life, saith the Lord; he that believeth on me, though he were dead, yet shall he live ; and whosoever liveth and believeth in me, shall never die.

Let not your heart be troubled : ye believe in God, believe also in me.

In my father's house are many mansions : If it were not so, I would have told you. I go to prepare a place for you.

And if I go and prepare a place for you, I will come again, and receive you unto myself; that where I am, there ye may be also.

If in this life only we have hope in Christ, we are of all men most miserable.

But now is Christ risen from the dead, and become the first fruits of them that slept.

For since by man came death, by man came also the resurrection from the dead.

For as in Adam all die, even so in Christ shall all be made alive.

PSALM.

Taken from Psalm xxxix.

Supt.—Lord, let me know my end, and the number of my days :

Chil.—That I may be certified how long I have to live.

Supt.—Behold, Thou hast made my days as it were a span long,

Chil.—And mine age is even as nothing in respect of Thee ;

Supt.—And verily every man living is altogether vanity.

Chil.—For man walketh in a vain shadow,

Supt.—And disquieteth himself in vain ;

Chil.—He heapeth up riches,

Supt.—And can not tell who shall gather them.

Chil.—And now, Lord, what is my hope ?

Supt.—Truly my hope is even in Thee.

Chil.—When Thou with rebukes dost chasten man for sin,

Supt.—Thou makest his beauty to consume away,

Chil.—Like as it were a moth fretting a garment :

Supt.—Every man therefore is but vanity.

Chil.—Hear my prayer, O Lord,

Supt.—And with Thine ears consider my calling :

Chil.—Hold not Thy peace at my tears :

Supt.—For I am a stranger with Thee, and a sojourner,

Chil.—As all my fathers were.

Supt.—O spare me a little, that I may recover my strength,

Chil.—Before I go hence, and be no more seen.

PRAYER.

OUR Father, Thou art our help in every time of need.—Our only hope is in Thee. —When the ties of earth break,—and those we love are borne from our sight—we look to Thee for strength.

It has pleased Thee to take to Thyself

our dear friend.—The places that knew *him*
but a little while ago—shall know *him* no
more.—But since Thou hast taken *him*—we
know it was the right and best time for *him*
to go.—Our hearts are filled with grief,—and
we turn to Thee for the help we need.—O
Lord, hear us, and be very near us,—and fill
our hearts with Thy peace.—Clasp us in
Thine arms—and lift us out of the gloom in
which we sit,—and lead us into the light of
Thy love.

We would not mourn as those who have
no hope.—All are in Thy care, the living and
the dead.—Those we love go from us, but
they go to Thee.—The dust goes back to the
dust it was,—but the soul goes to God who
gave it.

We thank Thee, our Father, for the friends
still spared to us.—We bless Thee for their
love.—And as they shall go one by one from
us,—not to come back,—may we who are still
left love each other more and more.—Bind
us, O God, in those ties, which death can not
break,—and bring us all in love to Thee.—
Grant us a hope that looks beyond the grave.
—And at the last lead us into that world
where there shall be no more death—that we
may praise Thee for ever,—through Jesus
Christ our Lord. *Amen.*

RURAL FESTIVAL.

Taken from Psalms xix., lxv., lxxiv.

The heavens declare the glory of God; and the firmament sheweth His handy work.

Day unto day uttereth speech, and night unto night sheweth knowledge.

The day is Thine, the night also is Thine; Thou hast prepared the light and the sun.

Thou hast set all the borders of the earth: Thou hast made summer and winter.

Thou crownest the year with Thy goodness; and Thy clouds drop fatness.

They drop upon the pastures of the wilderness; and the little hills rejoice on every side.

The pastures are clothed with flocks; the valleys are covered over with corn; they shout for joy, they also sing.

PSALM.

Taken from civ.

Supt.—O Lord, my God, Thou hast become exceeding glorious,

Chil.—Thou art clothed with majesty and honor.

Supt.—Thou deckest Thyself with light as it were with a garment,

Chil.—And spreadest out the heavens like a curtain.

Supt.—Thou layest the beams of Thy chambers in the waters,

Chil.—And makest the clouds Thy chariot;

Supt.—And walkest upon the wings of the wind.

Chil.—Thou layest the foundations of the earth,

Supt.—That it should not move at any time.

Chil.—Thou sendest the springs into the rivers, which run among the hills.

Supt.—Thou waterest the hills from above :

Chil.—The earth is filled with the fruit of Thy works.

Supt.—Thou bringest forth grass for the cattle,

Chil.—And green herb for the service of man.

Supt.—Thou appointest the moon for cer-tain seasons,

Chil.—And the sun knoweth his going down.

Supt.—O Lord, how manifold are Thy works ;

Chil.—In wisdom hast Thou made them all :

Supt.—The earth is full of Thy riches.

Chil.—The glorious majesty of the Lord shall endure for ever.

Supt.—The Lord shall rejoice in His works.

Chil —I will sing unto the Lord as long as I live;

Supt.—I will praise my God while I have my being.

Chil.—Praise Thou the Lord, O my soul.

PRAYER.

FATHER in Heaven, Thou hast given us the light of Thy works, and the light of Thy word.—And we thank Thee that both speak to us in a voice of love.

When we read Thy works, and know Thee as the Author,—we bow down and worship Thee,—for Thou art the same in Thy works as in Thy word.—Thine is the sun, the light and the sky;—Thine are the hills the trees and the grass;—Thine is the breath of flowers and the song of birds;—Thine is the smile on all we see;—Thine is this deep tide of life and joy;—and Thine the fair round world full of Thy riches.—They tell us how great and good Thou art.—They teach us to lift our hearts in love and trust to Thee.

Father in Heaven, we come to Thee now,—and while we feel the grandeur of Thy works,—may the thought of Thy goodness fill our hearts with joy.—And as we muse on this bright scene,—may it teach us of that brighter world, where joys shall never fade.

We pray Thee, O God, to keep us this

day without sin.—May the hours here passed
leave no stain upon our hearts.—May the
thought of Thy presence hallow all our joys.
—And may we go back to our homes—with
fresh strength for the work we have to do,—
with thanks to Thee for the fair world in
which we live,—thanks for the friends who
share with us its joys,—thanks for the hope
of meeting them in Heaven.—Father, hear
our prayer, and answer it through Jesus
Christ our Lord. *Amen.*

FOR AN ANNIVERSARY.

INTRODUCTORY SENTENCES.

Remember now thy Creator in the days of thy youth, while the evil days come not, nor the years draw nigh when thou shalt say, I have no pleasure in them.

What doth the Lord thy God require of thee, but to fear the Lord thy God, to walk in all His ways, and to love Him, and to serve the Lord thy God with all thy heart, and with all thy soul ?

O that such hearts were in you that you would love God, and keep all His laws, that it might be well with you all the days of your life.

PSALM.

Taken from Psalms lxiii., lxxxiv.

Supt.—O God, Thou art my God ;

Chil.—Early will I seek Thee,

Supt.—My soul thirsteth for Thee ; my flesh also longeth after Thee,

Chil.—In a barren and dry land where no water is.

Supt.—As long as I live will I magnify Thee in this manner.

Chil.—And lift my hands in Thy name.

Supt.—For Thy loving-kindness is better than the life itself :

Chil.—My lips shall praise Thee.

Supt.—O how amiable are Thy dwellings, Thou Lord of hosts !

Chil.—My soul hath a desire and longing to enter into the courts of the Lord.

Supt.—My heart and my flesh rejoice in the living God.

Chil.—Blessed are they that dwell in Thy house ;

Supt.—They will be always praising Thee.

Chil.—Blessed is the man whose strength is in Thee ;

Supt.—In whose heart are Thy ways,

Chil.—For one day in Thy court is better than a thousand.

Supt.—1 had rather be a door-keeper in the house of my God,

Chil.—Than to dwell in the tents of wickedness.

Supt.—For the Lord God is a light and defence :

Chil.—The Lord will give grace and worship ;

Supt.—And no good thing will He withhold from them that live a godly life.

Chil.—O Lord God of hosts, blessed is the man that putteth his trust in Thee.

PRAYER.

FATHER in Heaven, we bow with glad hearts before Thy throne,—and worship Thee, the High and Holy One.—We pray Thee to bless us who are met here this day.— Bless the friends who are with us,—and those we love who are not here.—Bless not only us, but all the world.—We thank Thee, O God, that Thou hast spared our lives to this hour.—May we be made better by the glad lessons which it brings to our souls.—In the midst of the young and the joyous, may our hearts be pure and right.

We thank Thee for the year that is gone,— and for all we have learned of Thee and our duty.—If we have not used Thy gifts as we ought,—we pray Thee to forgive us for all that is past.—And help us this day to give ourselves anew to Thy service.

We bless Thee for every gift of Thy love. —We bless Thee for the memory of the dead who died in the Lord,—and for the saints of all ages, who fought the good fight and kept the faith ;—we bless Thee for Christ, the dear Redeemer—and pray that we may have more and more of his spirit.

And O, our Father, we would not forget this day,—those who walk not in Thy paths. —We pray for those poor children, whose parents know Thee not.—Their homes are dark and drear.—Their hearts are sick and sad with sin.—Their minds have no ray of light from Thy word.—They are without

Thee, and without hope in the world.—Shew them Thy ways, O God.—Teach them Thy paths,—that they may know Thee, the Father, and love and serve Thee.

Be with us here to-day.—Bless all we do.— May all things be done to the praise of Thy name.—And if Thou shalt spare us to meet again,—may we come with hearts and minds stored with the rich gifts of Thy love.—And unto Thee, through Christ,—who lived and died for us,—be praise and glory, now and ever more. *Amen.*

PRAYERS.

AT TEACHERS MEETINGS.

————•●•————

I.

FATHER in Heaven, we implore Thy blessing, as we assemble here to-night — (to-
day.) As Teachers of Thy little ones, we
earnestly desire to be taught of Thee. Teach
us how we may best discharge our duties.
Teach us to be diligent in study, and frequent
in prayer. Give us patience to endure and
wisdom to govern, that the waywardness of
our pupils, and the trials of our calling may
not discourage us. Remembering the faith-
fulness of the Beloved Teacher, may we
labor hopefully, assured of the blessed result
of earnest effort, and cheered by the prospect
of children blest, and brought into Thy kingdom by our ministry.

Forgive us, if we have not been faithful to
our duties. Forgive us, if we have wished to
draw back from our labor. Forgive us, if,
by prayer, we have not sought aid and
guidance from Thee.

Ever help us, that as disciples of Jesus,
we may be good shepherds of the lambs of
his fold. On earth, may we be blessed with
the knowledge of their progress in love and
truth; and in Heaven, with joy and peace
87

may we learn, with them, diviner lessons, taught by the Great Teacher of souls. We ask it through Jesus Christ. *Amen.*

II.

WE bless Thee, Father of Mercies, that Thou hast called us to be the Teachers of Thy truth unto little children. We bless Thee that we may minister unto others, even as Christ hath ministered unto us. We bless Thee that in his name and stead, we may make known Thy holy will and word.

We pray that we who teach may be taught of Christ. We pray that we may so set forth the riches of his truth, as to win to him the hearts of those we teach. May we keep them in the kingdom to which they are born. Let us not grow weary of our service. If by reason of trial, or failure, we be tempted to leave our post of duty, may we resolve to be more faithful and steadfast, and labor with a new faith, and a better love.

May we be patient and long-suffering, gentle and forgiving. May we be meek and lowly, loving and merciful. May we, by example, as well as precept, guide the young in the way of pleasantness and peace.

O Father, help us to help them —teach us to teach them. Give unto us the spirit of the divine Teacher, Jesus, that we may lead the young to sit at his feet, and learn of him. Hear our prayer and grant us Thy blessing. We ask it in the name of him who taught us how to pray. *Amen.*

HYMNS.

"O come let us sing unto the Lord."
"The Lord is in His holy temple."

INTRODUCTORY.

8's and 7's M. **1.**

1 God is in His holy temple:
    Thoughts of earth be silent now,
While with reverence we assemble,
    And before His presence bow :
He is with us now and ever,
    When we call upon His name,
Aiding every good endeavor,
    Guiding every upward aim.

2 God is in His holy temple ;—
    In the pure and humble mind ;
In the reverent heart and simple;
    In the soul from sense refined :
Then let every low emotion,
    Banished far and silent be !
And our souls, in pure devotion,
    Lord, be temples worthy Thee!

7's and 5's M.   **2.**   Mrs. F. S. Osgood.

"Enter into His gates with thanksgiving."

1 Approach not the altar
    With gloom in thy soul,
Nor let thy feet falter
    At terror's control;
God loves not the sadness
    Of fear and mistrust;
O serve Him with gladness,
    The Loving and Just.

2 His bounty is tender,
    His being is love;
His smile fills with splendor
    The blue arch above;
Confiding, believing,
    O enter always
His courts with thanksgiving,
    His portals with praise!

3 Nor come to the temple
    With pride in thy mien;
But lowly and simple,
    In courage serene;
Bring meekly before Him
    The faith of a child;
Bow down and adore Him,
    With heart undefiled.

8's and 7's M.   **3.**

"Every good and every perfect gift is from above."

1 Gracious God, our heavenly Father!
    Meet and bless our school, we pray;
As in humble trust we gather,
    Teachers, scholars, here to-day.

2 Every joy, and every blessing,
   From Thy bounteous hand we own ;
   May Thy love, our souls possessing,
   Draw us nearer to Thy throne.

3 Weak, imperfect, tempted, erring,
   From thy precepts, Lord, we stray ;
   Let Thy spirit, from our wandering,
   Bring us back to virtue's way.

4 Humble, penitent, confiding,
   May we rest our hope in Thee ;
   In thy favor, Lord, abiding,
   In thy peace and purity.

8's M.   **4.**   CHARLES MACKAY.

"Unto thee O God do we give thanks."

1 Lord ! we are thankful for the air,
   For breath of life, and water fair,
   For morning burst, and noon-day light,
   And for the quiet of the night,
   For place in this glad world to be ;
   Lord ! we are thankful unto Thee.

2 For years and seasons as they run,
   For wintry cloud, and summer's sun,
   For seed-time, and the autumn store,
   That come in due time ever more,
   For flower and fruit, for herb and tree,
   Lord ! we are thankful unto Thee.

3 For sight, for touch, for taste, for smell,
   For sense of life ineffable,
   For health of mind, and strength of hand,
   For power to know and understand,
   For every joy we feel or see ;
   Lord ! we are thankful unto Thee.

4 For Conscience, and its voice of awe —
  Thy whisper when we break Thy law —
  For knowledge of Thy power divine,
  And wisdom, mighty as benign —
  For all we are, and hope to be,
  Lord ! we are thankful unto Thee.

L. M.   .   5.

"Our Father who art in heaven."

1 Great God, and wilt Thou condescend
  To be my Father and my Friend? —
  I but a child, and Thou so high,
  The Lord of earth, and air, and sky!

2 Art thou my Father? — Let me be
  A meek, obedient child to Thee;
  And try in every deed and thought,
  To serve and please Thee as I ought.

3 Art thou my Father? — I'll depend
  Upon the care of such a friend;
  And only wish to do, and be,
  Whatever seemeth good to Thee.

4 Art thou my Father? — Then at last,
  When all my days on earth are past,
  Send down and take me in Thy love,
  To be a better child above!

L. M.   6.

"The Lord is nigh unto all them that call upon Him."

1 God is so good that He will hear
    Whenever children humbly pray;
  He always lends a gracious ear
    To what the youngest child can say,

2 His own most holy book declares,
     That as a tender father will,
   He listens to our humble prayers,
     And what we ask will grant us still.

3 He loves to hear a grateful tongue
     Thank Him for all His mercies given;
   And when on earth His praise is sung,
     The cheerful notes are heard in heaven.

C. M.   7.   *MRS. H. J. LEWIS.

"Surely goodness and mercy shall follow me all the days of
my life."

1 Thanks, Father, that again our feet
     These sacred courts may press :
   Oh, let Thy spirit with us meet,
     And all our efforts bless !

2 How feeble, Lord, the noblest song
     Our youthful hearts can raise !
   Be Thou the theme, and sweet and strong
     Shall swell our hymn of praise.

3 Thy hand, through all our days and years,
     Has been our shield and guide :
   Through light and shade, through smiles and tears,
     What could we need beside?

4 And to Thy love, Thy sacred care,
     The future hours we give,
   All hallowed by the breath of prayer,
     Since by that breath we live.

5 Oh blessed Saviour ! in Thy name
     Let prayer and praise be given,
   And safely, from this mortal frame,
     Conduct our souls to heaven !

8.

"O come let us worship and bow down; let us kneel before the Lord our Maker."

Air Away to school

1 Away from home, to school we come,
Upon this holy day;
In faith and love, we look above,
And humbly praise and pray:
O, let this hour to God be given!
Let every heart be raised to Heaven!
And while in youth, we learn the truth,
May we the truth obey!

2 Our Teachers dear, we meet you here,
And share your faithful care;
O, may each heart its thanks impart,
In grateful, earnest prayer,
That God may crown, with joys above,
Your patient toils and works of love,
And that at last, life's changes past,
We all may meet you there.

3 O, let us now devoutly bow
Before our Father's face!
His will adore, His love implore,
To bless us all our days!
And humbly too, let us confess
Our folly, and our sinfulness:
Father, forgive! O, may we live
More worthy of Thy grace!

8 & 7's M.   ## 9.   ISAAC F. SHEPARD.

"O God, Thou art my God; early will I seek Thee."

Father, in Thy love awaking,
Let our souls their tribute bear,
And, while morning light is breaking,
Help us breathe our thankful prayer.

2 Through the night while sleep hath bound us,
   Thy kind love has kept us still,
   And Thine angel watches, round us,
   Guarded us from every ill.

3 Make us truthful, pure and lowly,
   In each deed, and word and thought;
   Fill our minds with precepts holy,
   That our Saviour's lips have taught.

4 And when all our days are ended,
   In the way of duty past,
   By Thy side, to Christ ascended,
   Fold us safe in Heaven at last!

7s. M. **10.** *MRS. M. A. H. SHULTS.

" My voice shall Thou hear in the morning."

1 Fair the Sabbath sun appears,
   Drying all night's dewy tears;
   Balmy is the summer air,
   And the birds are singing there.

2 No rude sound the morning greets,
   Hushed to quiet are the streets,
   And along in pleasant talk,
   Groups of happy children walk.

3 While, to hold communion sweet,
   At the Sabbath School we meet,
   Let us always careful be
   Every idle thought to flee.

4 We should love our teachers dear,
   For their care and kindness here,
   Keep the precepts we are taught,
   And be grateful as we ought.

S. M. **11.** Mrs. M. A. H. Shults.

"He took them up in his arms, and blessed them."

1 The Saviour, when on earth,
    Was gentle, meek and mild;
  He never coldly turned away,
    E'en from a little child.

2 When to him they were led,
    He blessed and called them his;
  He took them in his arms, and said,
    "Of such my kingdom is."

L. M. **12.**

"Order my steps in Thy word."

1 Assembled in our school once more,
  God's gracious blessing we'll implore:
  We meet to learn, and sing, and pray;
  May He be with us through this day.

2 We would be here when prayer begins,
  To seek the pardon of our sins;
  To ask the favor of the Lord,
  And pray to understand His word.

3 These Sabbath days will soon be o'er,
  And we shall come to school no more;
  We would not then endure the pain
  Of having spent our time in vain.

4 And when we meet on earth no more,
  May we to God, our Father, soar!
  And praise Him in more lofty strains,
  Where one eternal Sabbath reigns.

C. M.   **13.**

"They take delight in approaching to God."

1 We come in childhood's innocence,
   We come, as children, free!
We offer up, O God! our hearts
   In trusting love to Thee.

2 Well may we bend, in solemn joy,
   At Thy bright courts above;—
Well may the grateful child rejoice
   In such a Father's love.

3 We come not as the mighty come;
   Not as the proud we bow;
But as the pure in heart should bend,
   Seek we Thine altar now.

4 " Forbid them not," the Saviour said;—
   In holy rapture dumb, —
We hear the call — we seek Thy face, —
   Father! we come — we come!

14.

" In the morning I will direct my prayer unto Thee."

Air—" Mountain Maid's Invocation."

1   Come, come, come!
Don't delay, haste away,
To the Sabbath School to-day;
Here to meet, and to greet
   All in friendship sweet.
Come while yet the dews of morn
Nature's face with pearls adorn;
Be in time, rain or shine —
   Order is divine.

To the happy, happy school,
Joyous, joyous Sabbath School!
Be in time, rain or shine,
    Order is divine!

2   Come, come, come!
Not a tear — naught of fear
Nor of sorrow is found here;
Faces bright, tempers right,
    O, the happy sight!
Health and beauty all around,
And no harsh or jarring sound;
Light and free, full of glee,
    All is harmony.
O, the happy, happy school! ·
Joyous, joyous Sabbath-school, —
Light and free, full of glee,
    All is harmony.

3   Come, come, come!
Keep the way, do not stray,
'Tis the holy Sabbath day!
Hie along, join the throng,
    In their grateful song.
Hither come — nor decline
Bliss so rare and joys divine,
Pleasures pure, that endure,
    All may here secure.
O, the happy, happy school!
Joyous, joyous Sabbath-school!
Pleasures pure, that endure,
    All may here secure!

10 S. M.   **15.**

" Let them that love Him be as the sun, when he goeth forth in his might."

1 I'll awake at dawn on the Sabbath day,
For 'tis wrong to doze holy time away,
With my lesson learned, this shall be my rule,
Never to be late at the Sabbath School.

2 Birds awake betimes, every morn they sing,
None are tardy there, when the woods do ring;
So when Sunday comes, this shall be my rule,
Never to be late at the Sabbath School.

3 When the summer's sun wakes the flowers again,
They the call obey — none are tardy then;
Nor will I forget that it is my rule,
Never to be late at the Sabbath School.

6 & 4s. M.   **16.**   *R. C. WATERSTON.

" The Lord will bless His people with peace."

1 O God of Light and Love,
Look from Thy throne above,
And bliss impart;
While we in worship meet,
Holding communion sweet,
Make Thou our joy complete;
Bind heart to heart.

2 Great God, with heavenly power,
Fill Thou this sacred hour;
Make us as one:
May we united be,
Keep us from error free, —
True to Thy word and Thee, —
True to Thy Son.

C. M. **17.** *Mrs. M. A. H. Shults.

"Joy cometh in the morning."

1 Now far have fled the shades of night,
The sun in splendor reigns,
Pouring a flood of golden light
O'er mountains, vales and plains.

2 How pleasant and how fair the sight,
Morn's early beams disclose, —
The meadows green, the waters bright,
The dew-drop on the rose!

3 God of our lives! Thine is the care
Which bade the sun to shine,
And placed us in a world so fair,
Where all bright things are Thine.

4 O may we learn in all Thy ways,
Thy goodness still to see,
And in the morning of our days,
Give our young hearts to Thee!

L. M. **18.** *R. C. Waterston.

"God, even our own God shall bless us"

1 O Lord of Life! to Thee we pray,
Send down Thy spirit from above,
And fill, great Fount of truth, this day,
Each mind with light, each heart with love.

2 Thy children, Father, wilt Thou bless,
Conform our wills unto Thine own,
Give to Thy glorious word success,
And raise within each soul Thy throne.

L. M. **19.**

" Lead me in Thy truth and teach me."

1 Father in heaven, Thy ceaseless love
  Has brought us to this holy day ;
  Blest with Thy kindness from above,
  Another week has passed away.

2 Grant us, O Lord, a grateful heart
  To feel Thy goodness and obey :
  Ne'er may we from Thy love depart,
  Ne'er may we leave Thy heavenly way!

3 Grant us this day, a willing mind
  To learn what Thou wouldst have us do,
  And how we may Thy favor find,
  And love and serve each other too.

4 Thy happy children may we live,
  Thy happy children may we die ;
  To all may God, our Father, give
  A home of bliss beyond the sky.

L. M. **20.** JOHN PIERPONT.

"I laid me down and slept; I awaked; for the Lord sustained me."

1 O God, I thank Thee that the night
  In peace and rest hath passed away ;
  And that I see in this fair light,
  My Father's smile, that wakes the day.

2 Be Thou my Guide, and let me live
  As under Thine all-seeing eye :
  Supply my wants, my sins forgive,
  And make me happy when I die.

10s & 11s M.   **21.**

" Praise ye the Lord."

1 Let praise to the Lord, who made us, ascend;
   And let every heart be glad in its King ;
  The God whom we worship our songs will attend,
   And He will accept the pure off'ering we bring.

2 Be joyful, ye saints sustained by His might,
   And let your glad songs awake with each morn;
  For those who obey Him are still His delight —
   His hand with salvation the meek will adorn.

3 Then praise ye the Lord — prepare a new song,
   And let all His saints in full concert join ;
  With voices united the anthem prolong,
   And show forth His praises with music divine.

C. P. M   **22.**

" I will praise the name of God with a song." ˏ

1 Now let our hearts unite to raise
  A cheerful anthem to Thy praise,
    Our Father, God above ;
  Let music, as sweet incense rise
  In grateful accents to the skies,
    A chant of joy and love !

2 Thus brought again before Thy face,
  May we display each child-like grace
    To Thy heart-searching view
  O, help us, Father, to fulfil
  Thy ever wise and gracious will,
    In all we say and do !

S. P. M. **23.**

"Lord, I have loved the habitation of Thy house."

1   How sweet the Sabbath Home,
      Our Father, where we come
To read Thy word, and seek Thy face;
      And gladly we appear,
      To praise, and pray, and hear
How great Thy love, and rich Thy grace.

2   Thy peace attend our way,
      And may we, day by day,
Grow more and more like Christ, Thy Son,
      Until at last we come
      To our eternal home,
To dwell with Thee, most holy One.

S. H. M. **24.**

" Your Father knoweth what things ye have need of."

1 To Thee our wants are known,
   From Thee are all our powers ;
Accept what is Thine own,
   And pardon what is ours :
Our praises, Lord, and prayers, receive,
And to Thy words a blessing give.

2 O, grant that each of us
   Now met before Thee here,
May meet before Thee thus,
   When Thou and Thine appear :
To Thy blest presence may we come,
And dwell in an eternal home.

G O D.

8 & 7s. M. **25.**

"The glory of the Lord shall endure forever."

1 God is love; His mercy brightens
    All the path in which we move;
Bliss He wakes, and woe He lightens;
    God is wisdom, God is love.

2 Chance and change are busy ever;
    Man decays, and ages move,
But His mercy waneth never;
    God is wisdom God is love.

3 E'en the hour that darkest seemeth,
    Will His changeless goodness prove;
From the gloom his brightness streameth;
    God is wisdom, God is love.

4 He with earthly cares entwineth
    Hope and comfort from above;
Every where His glory shineth;
    God is wisdom, God is love.

C. M. **26.**

"He hath made every thing beautiful in its time."

1 There's not a tint that paints the rose,
    Or decks the lily fair,
Or streaks the humblest flower that grows,
    But God has placed it there.

2 There's not of grass a single blade,
    Or leaf of lowliest mien,
Where heavenly skill is not displayed,
    And heavenly wisdom seen.

3 There's not a star whose twinkling light
   Illumes the spreading earth;
   There's not a cloud, or dark or bright,
   But mercy gave it birth.

4 Then wake, my soul, and sing His name,
   And all his praise rehearse,
   Who spread abroad earth's glorious frame,
   And made the universe.

C. M.   **27.** *Mrs. E. Oakes Smith.

"God is love."

1 There is a song on every breeze,
   A language all around, —
   We hear it in the stirring trees,
   And from the verdant ground.

2 The blossom lifts its dewy eyes,
   And from its tiny cup,
   It sendeth to the listening skies
   Its adoration up.

3 With pluméd wing the little bird,
   Sings in the sheltering grove,
   And in that song a voice is heard,
   It says — " Our God is Love !"

4 O may that song in childhood's days,
   Within our hearts be found,
   And may we join that song of praise,
   Now heard from all around.

5 And thus on earth begin the song
   That swells in heaven above,
   Where ever bow the angel throng,"
   Who sing — " Our God is Love!

6 & 5s. M.   **28.**   *C. T. Brooks.

" The earth is full of the goodness of the Lord."

1 Morn amid the mountains!
  Lovely solitude!
  Gushing streams and fountains,
  Murmur, " God is good !"

2 Now the glad sun, breaking,
  Pours a golden flood;
  Deepest vales, awaking,
  Echo, " God is good !"

3 Hymns of praise are ringing
  Through the leafy wood;
  Songsters, sweetly singing,
  Warble, " God is good !"

4 Wake, and join the chorus,
  Child, with soul endued!
  He whose smile is o'er us —
  God, our " God, is good !"

29.

" Oh give thanks unto the Lord, for He is good!"

1   Anthems of gladness uniting to raise,
      Swell with your voices the chorus of praise;
  Sing and rejoice, and approach with thanksgiving,
    The throne that through ages eternal hath stood;
  For He who made earth, and gave life to all living,
    The greatest, the wisest, above all, is GOOD.
      Anthems of gladness uniting to raise,
      Swell with your voices the chorus of praise?

2 Praise to Jehovah! His name be adored!
   Praise the Creator! rejoice in the Lord!
Great is His power, beyond estimation;
  But greater His goodness, which gives life its
    worth;
His goodness is shown in the work of creation;
  And love to our Maker His love should call
    forth.
   Praise to Jehovah! His name be adored!
   Praise the Creator! rejoice in the Lord!

30.

8's. M.

"I will bless Thy name for ever and ever."

1 Blessed be Thy name forever,
 Thou of life the Guard and Giver!
 Thou canst shield Thy creatures sleeping,
 Dry the eyes of all the weeping:

2 Thou canst give the balm of gladness
 To the heart oppressed with sadness:
 Thou canst fill the poor and lowly
 With a joy serene and holy.

3 Thou who slumberest not nor sleepest,
 Blest are they Thou kindly keepest:
 God of life! that fade shall never,
 Blessed be Thy name forever!

31.

C. M.   *ALICE CARY.

"What wilt Thou have me to do?"

1 Dear Father, take me to Thy love,
 And ever keep me there,
That I may know Thy peace,—above,
 The reach of earthly care.

2 O, I can trust Him who provides
   The thirsty ground with dew,
Whose hand the world upholds and guides,
   For He is good and true.

3 For the same hand that smites with pain,
   And sends the wintry snows,
Will mould the frozen clod again
   Into the summer rose.

4 My soul is melted by that love,
   So tender and so true ;
I can but cry, my Lord and God,
   What wilt Thou have me do ?

PRAYER.

7's & 6's M.   **32.**

" Pray without ceasing."

1 Go, when the morning shineth,
   Go, when the noon is bright,
Go, when the eve declineth,
   Go, in the hush of night ;
Go, with pure mind and feeling,
   Cast earthly thought away,
And in thy chamber, kneeling,
   Do thou in secret pray.

2 O, not a joy nor blessing
   With this can we compare,
The power that God hath given us
   To pour our souls in prayer !
Whene'er thou pin'st in sadness,
   Before His footstool fall ;
Remember in thy gladness,
   His love who gave thee all.

S. M.

33.

"We know not what we should pray for as we ought."

1 Lord, teach us how to pray,
   And give us hearts to ask,
   Or all we seek, or think, or say,
   Will prove a weary task.

2 Thy holy Spirit send.
   Our bosoms to inspire;
   Then shall our praise to Thee ascend,
   With pure and warm desire.

P. M.   ## 34.   *Mrs. C. M. Sawyer

"Lord, teach us to pray."

1 Brothers, sisters, when the morning
   In the east is brightly dawning,
   And its golden rays are stealing
   Through our casement—Oh, then kneeling,
                    Let us pray !

2 When the light of day is waning,
   And its farewell hues are staining
   Every tree, and shrub, and flower,
   In that rich, that gorgeous hour,
                    Let us pray !

3 When her lips, fond caresses,
   On our cheek our mother presses,
   As her arms around us wreathing,
   She, the dear "good night" is breathing,
                    Let us pray !

4 Let us pray that on the morrow,
   God will shield our hearts from sorrow,
   And though life be ever near us —
   He is kind, and He will hear us,
                    When we pray !

GOD IN NATURE.

C. M.   **35.**   *ALICE CARY.

" The kingdom of God is within you."

1 O God, we see and feel Thy might,
   In all that nature shows ;
The strong wind's breath, the tender light
   That opes the joyous rose.

2 But life, with what we call its laws,
   And all things fair and bright,
Are curtains which Thy mercy draws,
   To shield us from the light.

3 We falter, when we try to seek
   The world which these conceal,
We stammer, when we fain would speak
   The reverence that we feel.

4 We pray not now, for Thee to give
   That heaven which shall appear:
We only cry — help us to live
   Within Thy kingdom here !

S. M.   **36.**   *MRS. H. J. LEWIS.

" The Lord hath made all thi ngs."

1 On the blue, tranquil sea,
   That laves the shining san d,
On every budding shrub and tree,
   We trace our Father's hand.

2 The song of every bird
   That makes the woods rejoice,
Seems to our heart, whenever heard,
   An echo of His voice,

3 The mountains grand and still,
    The stars amid the skies,
  The sparkling of the tiniest rill,
    Thy gracious hand supplies.

4 The holy hush of night,
    That moves the soul to prayer,
  The ruddy tints of morning light;
    All tell us of Thy care.

5 Since all to Thee we owe,
    We will withhold no part,
  But yield Thee, with a grateful glow,
    Each young and trusting heart.

L. M.   **37.**   *Mrs. C. M. Sawyer

" My son, give me thine heart."

1 Give me thy heart, O thoughtless youth,
    Ere yet the evil days draw near !
  O, early seek the ways of truth,
    Ere hope grow dim, ere life be drear !

2 Give me thine heart ! The yoke I lay
    Upon thy youthful neck is light ;
  My burden grows from day to day,
    More dear to sense, more fair to sight !

3 Come to me now ! The crown I press
    Upon thy brow, hath not a thorn ;
  A crown so rare, to soothe and bless,
    No royal head hath ever worn !

4 Come to me now ! This hour, decide,—
    And be thine offering full and free :
  Oh, for His sake, who for thee died,
    My wandering child, come home to me !

C. M.   **38.**

" As the hart panteth after the water-brooks, so panteth my soul after Thee, O God."

1 The wild flower drinks the morning dew,
      And greets the breezes free;
   The pure in heart their strength renew,
      From Thee, my God, from Thee!

2 The tired bird seeks at night her nest,
      Hid in the sheltering tree;
   So longs the weary soul to rest
      On Thee, my God, on Thee!

3 The barque, by storms and tempests driven,
      To its safe port would flee;
   So turns the spirit sorely riven,
      To Thee, my God, to Thee!

4 Light of the worn and weary mind,
      Joy of the glad and free,
   O grant me sweet repose to find,
      In Thee my God, in Thee!

C. M.   **39.**

" O God, who is like unto Thee?"

1 None is like God, who reigns above,
      So great, so pure, so high,
   None is like God, whose name is love,
      And who is always nigh.

2 In all the earth there is no spot
      That does not claim His care:
   We cannot go where God is not,
      For He is every where.

3 He is our best and kindest Friend,
  And guards us night and day:
To all our wants He will attend,
  And answer when we pray.

4 O, if we love Him as we ought,
  And on His grace rely,
We shall be joyful at the thought
  That God is ever nigh !

JESUS.

8's, 7's & 4's M.   **40.**

" Behold the Lamb of God, which taketh away the sin of the world !"

1 Children, hear the melting story
    Of the Lamb that once was slain;
  'Tis the Lord of life and glory ;
    Shall he plead with you in vain ?
      O receive him,
    And salvation now obtain.

2 Yield no more to sin and folly,
    So displeasing in his sight:
  Jesus loves the pure and holy ;
    They alone are his delight:
      Seek his favor,
    And your hearts to him unite.

3 All your sins to him confessing,
    Who is ready to forgive ;
  Seek the Saviour's richest blessing,
    On his precious name believe:
      He is waiting ;
    Will you not his grace receive ?

THE LORD OUR SHEPHERD.

7's M.   **41.**   *HENRY C. LEONARD.

" The Lord is my Shepherd."

1 Shepherd of the holy hills,
    We, thy lambs, with tender feet,
Follow thee beside the rills,
    And through pastures fair and sweet.

2 Thou dost hear us when we cry;
    Thou dost watch us when alone:
When we faint, thou drawest nigh,
    Soothing us with winning tone.

3 Thus through all our earthly way,
    Be our guard and only guide;
Draw us from the evil way;
    Keep us ever by thy side.

4 And when fall the shades of night
    On the paths we tread below,
Take us to the fields of light,
    Where the living waters flow.

11's M.   **42.**

" I am the good Shepherd."

1 ·The Lord is our Shepherd, our Guardian and Guide;
Whatever we want he will kindly provide;
His care and protection his flock will surround;
To them will his mercies forever abound.

2 The Lord is our shepherd; what, then, shall we
     fear?
Shall dangers affright us while help is so near?
O, no: when he calls us we'll walk through the
     vale,
The shadow of death, but our hearts shall not fail.

3 Afraid, of ourselves, to pursue the dark way,
  Thy rod and thy staff be our comfort and stay:
  We know, by thy guidance, when once it is past,
  To life and to glory it brings us at last.

8's & 7's M. **43.**

." Follow me."

1 Jesus Christ, my Lord and Saviour,
   Once became a child like me;
  O that in my whole behavior
   He my pattern still may be.

2 If my feelings are not holy,
   Pride and passion dwell within;
  But the Lord was meek and lowly,
   And was never known to sin.

3 While I'm often vainly trying
   Some new pleasure to possess, —
  He was always self-denying,
   Patient in his deep distress.

4 Lord, assist a feeble creature,
   Guide me by thy word of truth;
  Condescend to be my teacher
   Through my childhood and my youth.

THE LAMBS OF JESUS.

L. M. **44.**

" Feed my lambs."

1 The Lambs of Jesus! who are they
  But children that believe and pray —
  That keep God's laws, and ask His grace,
  And seek a heavenly dwelling place?

2 The Lambs of Jesus! they are meek,
   The words of peace and truth they speak
   To all God's creatures they are kind,
   And, like their Lord, of gentle mind.

3 The Lambs of Jesus! O that we
   Might of that blesséd number be
   Lord take us early to Thy love,
   And lead us to the fold above.

7's M.   **45.**   W. H. FURNESS, D. D.

"Lead me in the way everlasting."

1 Feeble, helpless, how shall I
   Learn to live, and learn to die?
   Who, O God, my guide shall be?
   Who shall lead Thy child to Thee?

2 Blessed Father, gracious One!
   Thou hast sent Thy holy Son;
   He will give the light I need,
   He my trembling steps will lead.

3 Through this world, uncertain, dim,
   Let me ever lean on him;
   From his precepts wisdom draw,
   Make his life my solemn law.

4 Thus in deed, and thought, and word,
   Led by Jesus Christ the Lord,
   In my weakness, — thus shall I
   Learn to live and learn to die.

CHRISTMAS.

6's & 5's M.   46.   Wᴍ Cʀᴏsᴡᴇʟʟ, D. D.

"Waiting for the coming of our Lord Jesus Christ."

1 With lamps trimmed and burning,
    The Church, on her way
To meet Thy returning,
    O bright King of day!
Goes forth and rejoices,
    Exulting and free,
And sends from all voices
    Hosannas to thee!

2 She casts off her sorrows,
    To rise and to shine
With the lustre she borrows,
    O Saviour! from thine.
Look down, for thine honor,
    O Lord! and increase,
In thy mercy upon her,
    The blessing of peace.

3 Her children with trembling,
    Await without fear,
Till the time of assembling
    Before thee draws near;
When free from all sadness,
    And sorrow and pain,
They shall meet thee in gladness
    And glory again.

C. M.   47.   Wᴍ. Cʀᴏsᴡᴇʟʟ, D.D.

" Thou shalt call his name Jesus, for he shall save his people from their sins."

1 Now raise your joyous songs again,
    Your wasting torches trim!
The chief of all the sons of men,
    Shall we not welcome him?

2 Fill all his courts with sacred songs,
   And from the temple wall,
Wave garlands o'er the joyful throngs
   That crowd his festival!

3 And still more freshly in the mind,
   Store up the hopes sublime,
Which then were born for all mankind,
   So blessèd was the time:

4 And underneath these hallowed caves
   A Saviour will be born,
In every heart that him receives,
   On this triumphal morn!

8's, 7's & 4's M.   **48.**

"There were shepherds abiding in the field keeping watch over their flocks by night."

1 Shepherds in the field abiding,
   Watching o'er their flocks by night,
Heard the message, joy betiding,
   Of the angel clad in light:—
      " Fear no evil!
Christ the Lord is born to-night!"

2 And the heavenly host, appearing,
   Praised the Lord in loftiest strain!
Human hearts with mercy cheering,
   Thus proclaimed the Saviour's reign:—
      " Give God glory!
Peace on earth, good will to men!"

3 Wise men, in the East, adoring
   In the star an unknown King;
Guided by its light, exploring
   Where their treasures they might bring,—
      Came to Jesus—
In the manger saw the King!

4 Children, see yet shining o'er us,
   The bright star of Bethlehem's plain!
Children, join the heavenly chorus,
   Sing the angels' song again:—
      " Give God glory!
   Peace on earth, good will to men!"

6's & 5's M.   **49.** G. W. Bethune, D. D.

" Unto you is born this day in the city of David, a Saviour,
who is Christ the Lord."

1 Hark, the angels, singing,
   Wake the happy morn,
Joyful tidings bringing,
   " Christ, the Lord, is born!
In a lowly manger—
   This shall be the sign —
See the new-born stranger,
   Hail the Babe divine!"

2 Sisters dear, and brothers,
   Sing, O sing away!
This, above all others,
   Is the childrens' day.
Hear its blessed story:
   " Once, as young as we,
Christ, the Prince of Glory,
   Slept on Mary's knee."

3 Where's a chorus meeter,
   For his advent here?
Where a carol sweeter,
   To his gentle ear?
None can come so near him,
   Him, the undefiled,
None so love and fear him,
   As a Christian child.

4 In the highest regions,
　　On his throne above,
All the ransomed legions,
　　Sing his matchless love :
But of all who greet him,
　　With triumphant song,
Little children meet him
　　In the greatest throng.

5 Let us then pursue him,
　　In the way he trod,
Ever calling to him —
　　"Blessed Son of God !
Once in childhood's weakness,
　　Christ, like us, wert thou;
O, in love and meekness,
　　Make us like thee now !"

C. M

50.

E. H. SEARS.

" And suddenly there was with the angel a multitude of the heavenly host praising God."

1 Calm on the listening ear of night
　　Come heaven's melodious strains,
Where wild Judea stretches far
　　Her silver-mantled plains.

2 Celestial choirs, from courts above,
　　Shed sacred glories there ;
And angels, with their sparkling lyres,
　　Make music on the air.

3 The answering hills of Palestine
　　Send back the glad reply,
And greet, from all their holy heights,
　　The day-spring from on high.

4 Light on thy hills, Jerusalem!
The Saviour now is born!
And bright on Bethlehem's joyous plains
Breaks the first Christmas morn.

51. E. H. Chapin, D. D.

" Glory be to God in the highest, and on earth peace, good
will toward men."

1 Hark! hark! with harps of gold,
What anthem do they sing?
The radiant clouds have backward rolled,
And angels smite the string.
"Glory to God!"—bright wings
Spread glistening and afar,
And on the hallowed rapture rings
From circling star to star.

2 "Glory to God!" repeat
The glad earth and the sea;
And every wind and billow fleet,
Bears on the jubilee.
Where Hebrew bard hath sung,
Or Hebrew seer hath trod,
Each holy spot has found a tongue:
" Let glory be to God!"

3 Soft swells the music now
Along the shining choir,
And every seraph bends his brow,
And breathes above his lyre.
What words of heavenly birth
Thrill through our hearts again,
And fall like dew-drops on the earth?
" Peace and good-will to men!"

4 Soft! — yet the soul is bound
   With rapture like a chain:
Earth, vocal, whispers them around,
   And heaven repeats the strain.
   Sound, harps, and hail the morn
   With every golden string; —
For unto you this day is born
   A Saviour and a King!

7's M.   **52.** *Mrs. L. H. Sigourney

"He that followeth me shall have the light of life."

1 Holy Saviour, — thou wert laid
   In the humble manger's shade, —
   Choosing out thy lot below
   With the sons of want and woe;

2 Teaching wisdom's heavenly words
   By the lilies and the birds, —
   Seeking peace on earth to give,
   Dying that the lost may live:

3 Thou who patiently didst teach
   Lowly thought, and gentle speech,
   Deign to hear the hymn we raise —
   Take this tribute of our praise.

4 Let us try with earnest mind
   All our faults to leave behind,
   Meekly learning day by day,
   How to work and how to pray.

5 Grant us all in love to dwell,
   Truth to keep, and anger quell: —
   Be our friend whate'er betide —
   Blessed Saviour, be our guide!

7's M.   **53.**   *JOHN PIERPONT.

" And he took them up in his arms, put his hands upon them and blessed them."

1 Once were little children led
To the Lord, that, on their head
He his holy hand might lay,
And God's blessing on them pray.

2 They, who stood around, reproved
Those who brought them, but he loved,
Round his knees to see them stand,
For a blessing from his hand.

3 " Ne'er, Oh, ne'er forbid," said he,
"Little ones to come to me :
Let them all to me be given;
For of such as these is heaven."

4 On this joyous Christmas morn,
Was the children's Saviour born ;
Children, then, shall on this day,
Sing aloud their hymns, and pray.

5 Pray that his kind hand, so blest,
On their heads may ever rest,
That his spirit, from above,
All their souls may fill with love;

6 And that, as the Father's grace
Shone, reflected from his face,
So may their young faces shine,
With the Saviour's love divine !

THE NEW YEAR.

L. M.   54.   *EDWARD   NORTH.

"We spend our days as a tale that is told."

1 Good-by, Old Year, a fond good-by!
    We thank God for each sunny day,
    Whose gifts of joy and beauty, lie
    Still fresh in thought, to bless our way.

2 Thou hast seen those we love, Old Year,
    Pass as the light goes out at even,
    And we are left to linger here,
    While our hearts' treasures are in heaven.

3 Welcome, New Year — a welcome warm!
    Thy voice to joy or grief may call;
    Yet we will greet the calm or storm,
    Since God shall be with us through all!

4 If we but look with faith's clear sight,
    Life's griefs are blessings in disguise;
    And clouded years, when lived aright,
    Deepen the rapture of the skies!

7's & 6's M.   55.   *R. F. FULLER.

"But Thou art the same, and Thy years shall have no end."

1 How many warm hearts beating,
    And happy faces here,
    Are met, with merry greeting,
    To hail the new-born year!

2 Why greet the new year gladly,
    When we so little know
    What clouds may gather sadly,
    To bring us grief and woe?

3 Hope sings the song of heaven,
　And fills the heart with cheer;
And Faith, that God has given,
　Still hails the coming year.

4 Young hearts, away with sadness!
　Throw off the yoke of fear,
And welcome now with gladness,
　The new and happy year!

5 To holy, high endeavor,
　We pledge ourselves anew,
And onward, still forever,
　The heavenly path pursue!

L. M.　　　　　　56.　　*SALLIE M. BRYAN.

" Thou crownest the year with Thy goodness."

1 Another year comes from above,
　To prove our Father's constant love;
He sends the sunlight and the flowers,
And shields us when the winter lowers.

2 And from the regions of the sky,
He sent His Holy Son to die,
That he might take our sins away,
And lead us in the living way.

3 How we, from sin and error won,
Should love the Father and the Son,
And strive in their full love to rest,
Where all is beautiful and blest!

4 Then shall this year, that comes to bring
So many mercies on its wing,
Leave those who go, where peace is given,
And those who stay, more worthy heaven!

EASTER.

C. M.   **57.**

" Christ is risen from the dead."

1 Again the Lord of life and light
   Awakes the kindling ray;
Unseals the eyelids of the morn,
   And pours increasing day.

2 O what a night was that which wrapt
   The heathen world in gloom!
O what a sun, which broke, this day,
   Triumphant from the tomb!

3 This day be grateful homage paid,
   And loud hosannas sung;
Let gladness dwell in every heart,
   And praise on every tongue.

58.

" He is not here, but is risen."

1 " The Lord is risen indeed!"
   Attending angels hear;
Up to the courts of Heaven, with speed,
   The joyful tidings bear.

2 Then wake your golden lyres,
   And strike each cheerful chord;
Join, all ye bright celestial choirs,
   To sing the risen Lord.

59.

"Death hath no more dominion over him."

1 Lift your glad voices in triumph on high,
 For Jesus hath risen, and man cannot die:
Vain were the terrors that gathered around him,
 And short the dominion of death and the grave;
He rose from the fetters of darkness that bound
 him,
  Resplendent in glory, to live and to save:
  Loud was the chorus of angels on high,
  The Saviour hath risen, and man shall not
   die.

2 Glory to God in full anthems of joy,
 The being He gave us death can not destroy:
Sad were the life we must part with to-morrow,
 If tears were our birth-right, and death were
  our end;
But Jesus hath cheered the dark valley of sorrow,
 And bade us, immortal, to heaven ascend:
  Lift then your voices in triumph on high,
  For Jesus hath risen, and man shall not die.

BAPTISM.

C. M.

60.

" He shall feed his flock like a Shepherd."

1 See, the kind Shepherd, Jesus stands
  With all-engaging charms; •
 Hark, how he calls the tender lambs,
  And folds them in his arms!

2 "Permit them to approach," he cries,
  "Nor scorn their humble name;
For 'twas to bless such souls as these
  The Lord of glory came.

3 He leads them to the heavenly streams,
  Where living waters flow;
And guides them to the fruitful fields,
  Where trees of knowledge grow.

4 The feeblest lambs amid the flock,
  Shall be the Shepherd's care;
While folded in the Saviour's arms,
  They're safe from every snare.

L. M.   **61.**   *James Lombard.

"Suffer little children to come unto me."

1 Most Holy God, we bring to Thee
  These little ones that Thou hast given,
And ask, that they may ever be
  Thy children here, and Thine in Heaven.

2 O, take them in Thy gracious arms,
  And fold them fondly to Thy breast;
And there, secure from all alarms,
  Serene and sweet shall be their rest.

3 O, save them from the world's control,
  And keep their feet in that sure way
Where sin can never soil the soul,
  And life is but a pleasant day.

4 Dear Father, let Thy blessing now
  Descend like water from above,
That those who at Thine altar bow,
  May be baptized in Thy pure love!

C. M. **62.** Samuel Longfellow.

"And he saw the heavens opened, and the Spirit like a dove descending upon him."

1 Now, with baptismal waters touched,
   Thy children, Father, see!
While heart, and soul, and mind, and strength,
   They consecrate to Thee!

2 Send down on them Thy holy dove,
   Thy Spirit undefiled;
Be each in faith, and hope, and love,
   Thy well-beloved child!

3 O, help them in the wilderness
   To conquer doubt and sin;
To see above them still Thy peace,
   And hear Thy voice within!

S. M. **63.** Wm. Croswell, D.D.

"Blessed are they dwell in Thy house."

1 The sparrow finds a home,
   The little bird a nest;
Deep in Thy dwelling, Lord, they come,
   And fold themselves to rest.

2 And shall we be afraid,
   Thy little ones, to come,
And find within Thine altar's shade,
   And 'neath Thy wings, a home?

3 Here guard us as Thine eye,
   Here keep us without spot,
That when the spoiler passeth by,
   His hand may touch us not.

4 Here nerve our souls with might,
 Here nurse them with Thy love,
Here plume them for their final flight,
 To blessedness above!

***

AFTER BAPTISM.

64.

" Thou, O God, hast heard my vows."

1 O happy bond, that seals my vows
 To Him who claims my highest love!
Let cheerful anthems fill His house,
 While to His altar now I move.

2 'Tis done—the holy work is done;
 I am my Lord's, and He is mine;
He drew me, and I followed on,
 Glad to confess the voice divine.

3 High heaven, that heard the solemn vow,
 That vow renewed shall daily hear;
Till in life's latest hour I bow,
 And bless in death a bond so dear.

***

HEAVEN.

P. M.

65.

" It doth not yet appear what we shall be."

1 There is a happy land,
 Far, far away,
Where saints in glory stand,
 Bright, bright as day;
Oh, how they sweetly sing,
Worthy is the Saviour King,
Loud let his praises ring,
 Praise, praise for aye!

2 Come to that happy land,
  Come, come away;
Why will ye doubting stand,
  Why still delay?
Oh, we shall happy be,
When, from sin and sorrow free,
Lord, we shall live with thee,
  Blest, blest for aye.

3 Bright, in that happy land,
  Beams every eye;
Kept by a Father's hand,
  Love can not die.
Oh, then, to glory run,
Be a crown and kingdom won,
And, bright above the sun,
  We reign for aye.

C. M.   **66.**   *Mary Noel Meigs.

" At thy right hand there are pleasures forever more."

1 'Twere vain to think what Heaven will be,
  And wish that we could know,
If lovely things will charm us there,
  Such as we prize below.

2 For mortal eye hath never seen,
  Nor mortal eye shall see,
The love and joy laid up in store
  With Christ eternally.

3 Heaven is a holy, happy place,
  And 'tis enough to know,
Where angels sing, and Jesus dwells,
  Unfailing pleasures flow.

7's M. **67.**

"These are they which came out of great tribulation."

1 Who are these in bright array,
    This exulting, countless throng,
Round the altar, night and day,
    Singing their triumphant song?
"Worthy is the Lamb, once slain,
    Blessing, honor, glory, power,
Wisdom, riches, to obtain,
    New dominion every hour."

2 These through fiery trials trod;
    These from great affliction came;
Now, before the throne of God,
    Sealed with his almighty name;
Clad in raiment pure and white,
    Victor-palms in every hand,
Through their great Redeemer's might,
    More than conquerors they stand.

3 Hunger, thirst, disease, unknown,
    On immortal fruits they feed;
Them the Lamb, amidst the throne,
    Shall to living fountains lead:
Joy and gladness banish sighs;
    Perfect love dispels all fears;
And forever from their eyes
    God shall wipe away their tears.

S. M. **68.** *Mrs. M. A. H. Shults.

"We have a building of God, a house not made with hands, eternal in the heavens."

1 Now o'er earth's smiling face
    Our eyes delighted roam,
But this is not our dwelling-place,
    We have another home.

2 We look beyond this sphere,
    To one more bright and pure ;
Where sin can never cause a tear,
    Nor pain the heart endure ;

3 Where those that we have loved
    In happiness shall meet,
Their radiant brows with glory crowned,
    Shall bend at Jesus' feet.

4 This faith be our defence
    From fear, when death shall come,
Whom God will send to call us hence,
    To heaven, our other home.

SICKNESS.

L. M   **69.** *Mrs. M. A. H. Shults.

" He whom thou lovest is sick."

1 Father, while here once more we raise
To Thee our morning hymn of praise,
We miss one dear, familiar face,
One form from its accustomed place.

2 That form, bowed down with illness lies,
While shadows dim the heavy eyes,
And pale the face, with bitter pain,
And human skill is all in vain.

3 Oh Great Physician ! be Thou near,
The drooping sufferer to cheer ;
Around the bed Thy balm distil,
The fainting frame with life to fill.

4 Father, give health and strength again
To one so helpless now with pain ;
Restore the dear, familiar face,
Once more to its accustomed place

11's M.   **70.**

"For to me to live is Christ, and to die is gain."

1 I would not live alway; I ask not to stay
  Where storm after storm rises dark o'er the way;
  I would not live alway; no, welcome the tomb,
  Since Jesus hath lain there, I dread not its gloom.

2 Who, who would live alway, away from his God,
  Away from yon heaven, that blissful abode,
  Where the rivers of pleasure flow over bright plains,
  And the noontide of glory eternally reigns:

3 Where the saints of all ages in harmony meet,
  Their Saviour and Brother transported to greet;
  While the anthems of rapture unceasingly roll,
  And the smile of the Lord is the life of the soul.

DEATH.

8's & 7's M.   **71.**   R. C. WATERSTON.

"The Lord gave, and the Lord hath taken away."

1 One sweet flower has drooped and faded,
    One sweet infant voice has fled;
  One fair brow the grave has shaded,
    One dear school-mate now is dead!

2 She has gone to heaven before us;
    But she turns and waves her hand,
  Pointing to the glories o'er us,
    In that happy spirit-land.

3 May our footsteps never falter
    In the path that she has trod;
  Let us worship at the altar
    Where she gave her heart to God.

4 God, our Father, watch above us,
    Keep us from all error free;
Do Thou guard, and guide, and love us,
    Till, like her, we go to Thee.

C. M.   **72.**   JOHN G. WHITTIER.

"Come up hither."

1 Another hand is beckoning us,
    Another call is given,
And glows once more with angel steps
    The path which reaches Heaven.

2 The blessings of her quiet life
    Fell on us as the dew;
And good thoughts, where her footsteps fell,
    Like fairy blossoms grew.

3 Alone, unto our Father's will,
    One thought hath reconciled,
That He, whose love is more than ours,
    Has taken home His child.

4 Fold her, O Father, in Thine arms,
    And let her henceforth be,
A messenger of love between
    Our human hearts and Thee!

L. M.   **73.**   *MRS. M. A. H. SHULTS.

" He cometh forth like a flower and is cut down."

1 Like a fresh rose some hand has torn,
    When opening to the morning sky;
Such was the fate of her we mourn,
    One who was early called to die.

2 Though beauty from the rose depart,
   The air its fragrance still retains,
And cherished long within the heart
   The memory of the loved remains.

3 She smiled on Death, who softly came
   To seal her eyes in gentle sleep,
And take her from disease and pain:
   For her we need no longer weep.

4 Sweet peace is on her placid brow,
   Her voice to songs of praise is given,
Her home is with the angels now,
   Our dear young sister is in heaven.

6 & 5s M.   **74.**

" Of such is the kingdom of heaven."

1 Saviour, now receive him
   To Thy bosom mild;
For with Thee we leave him,
   Gentle, blessed child!

2 When Thine arms enfold him,
   To Thy loving breast,
Let our thought behold him
   In angelic rest.

3 We yield what Thou hast given,
   Thou who givest all!
The beautiful to Heaven,
   At Thy holy call;

8's & 7's M.   **75.**   PHŒBE CARY.

" He shall gather the lambs with his arm and carry them
in his bosom."

1 One who all our deep affection,
   All our pleading could not save,
   Now is gone, and dust is scattered
   On his beauty in the grave.

2 Fairest of the lambs immortal,
   In the Shepherd's bosom borne,
   To green pastures, and still waters,
   Is the little one we mourn.

3 Here, forgetting in our sorrow
   What the Father knows above,
   That the Saviour's arm is stronger
   Than the clasp of human love.

4 And that little children taken,
   Go, ere evil days begin,
   Through the gates of death to Jesus,
   With no sorrow and no sin !

C. M.   **76.**   *ALICE CARY.

" Not one of them is forgotten before God."

1 Our Father notes the sparrow's fall,
   He is our guard and guide;
   Without Him who is life to all,
   Our friend could not have died.

2 His grace the same, the same His power:
   He claims our love and trust,
   Whether He make of dust a flower,
   Or change the flower to dust.

3 He gives on land and sea, to all,
   The strength to bear or pray;
He blights the leaves when they should fall,
   Or lights the hills with May!

C. M.   **77.**   Mrs. Hemans.

"Is it well with the child? It is well."

1 Calm on the bosom of thy God,
   Young spirit, rest thee now!
E'en while with us thy footstep trod,
   His seal was on thy brow.

2 Dust, to its narrow house beneath!
   Soul, to its place on high!
They that have seen thy look in death,
   No more may fear to die.

3 Lone are the paths, and sad the bowers,
   Whence thy meek smile is gone;
But, O, a brighter home than ours,
   In Heaven, is now thine own!

S. M.   **78.**

" Precious in the sight of the Lord is the death of His
saints."

1 For all Thy saints, O God,
   Who strove in Christ to live,
Who followed him, obeyed, adored,
   Our grateful hymns receive.

2 For all Thy saints, O God,
   Accept our thankful cry,
Who counted Christ their great reward,
   And strove in him to die.

3 For this Thy name we bless,
  And humbly beg that we
May follow them in holiness,
  And live and die in Thee.

EVENING.

C. M.   **79.**   *Mrs. C. M. Sawyer.

" Thou shalt lie down, and thy sleep shall be sweet."

1 Lord, wilt Thou guide an infant heart,
    That fain would turn to Thee ?
  Thou carest for the sparrow's fall,
    And wilt remember me!

2 When evening comes, the hour of prayer—
    The time good children love ;
  How sweet to leave my childish play,
    And lift my thoughts above !

3 Then o'er my free, glad spirit comes
    A happiness so pure,
  To gain it, days of grief and pain
    Were little to endure.

4 I'll bless the hour I first was taught
    To bend the lowly knee,
  And from the depths of my young heart
    To lisp a prayer to Thee!

11's M.   **80.**   *Anne C. Botta.

"There shall be no night there."

1 On the swift-flying hours, another bright day,
  With its smiles and its tears has vanished away ;
  O Thou who dost number our days as they flee,
  May each that departs bring us nearer to Thee!

2 On the wide sea of life our barques will be tossed,
   And the sweet ties that bind us be broken and lost:
   O Father in Heaven, be our guide to that shore
   Where night never cometh, where partings are o'er.

L. M.   **81.**   PIERPONT.

"Thou wilt keep him in perfect peace whose mind is stayed on Thee."

1 Another day its course has run,
   And still, O God, Thy child is blest;
For Thou hast been by day my sun,
   And Thou wilt be by night my rest.

2 Sweet sleep descends mine eyes to close;
   And now when all the world is still,
I give my body to repose,
   My spirit to my Father's will.

L. M.   **82.**

"Abide with us, for it is toward evening."

1 Lord, I have passed another day,
   And come to thank Thee for Thy care:
Forgive my faults in work and play,
   And listen to my evening prayer.

2 Thy favor gives me daily bread,
   And friends, who all my wants supply;
And safely now I rest my head,
   Preserved and guarded by Thine eye.

3 Look down in pity, and forgive
   All I have said or done amiss
And help me every day I live,
   To serve Thee better than in this.

4 Now, while I speak, be pleased to take
   A helpless child beneath Thy care;
And condescend, for Jesus' sake,
   To listen to my evening prayer.

8's & 7's M.   **83.**

"Let my prayer be as the evening sacrifice."

1 Through the day Thy love hath spared us,
   Now we lay us down to rest;
Through the silent watches guard us,
   Let no foe our peace molest;
Father, Thou our guardian be,
Sweet it is to trust in Thee.

2 Pilgrims here on earth and strangers,
   Dwelling in the midst of foes,—
Us and ours preserve from dangers,
   In Thine arms let us repose,
And, when life's short day is past,
Rest with Thee in heaven at last.

CLOSE OF SCHOOL IN SUMMER.

8's & 7's M.   **84.**   *THEODORE TILTON.

" Thou Lord. hast made me glad through Thy works."

1 The year's last song, and then we part!
   How swiftly time is winging!
But sweet are farewells of the heart,
   When they are said in singing!—
The roses climb the garden wall;
   The buds are past their blowing;
The summer's breezy voices call,
   And we must now be going!

2 The thrush is on her trembling nest,
  Which every wind is swaying;
And every robin shows his breast,
  While we are here delaying!
The bees have set their pipes in tune
  On every head of clover;
And we must haste to hear them soon,
  Or summer will be over!

3 To-day the birds on every bough
  Their Sabbath chimes are ringing;—
The Lord is in his temple now—
  We praise Him with our singing!
Without, within, the voices chord!
  One praise we all are giving—
To Thee! the Ever-Loving Lord,
  To Thee! the Ever-Living!

4 O God of every human heart,
  And every heart's pure feeling,
We love and praise Thee as Thou art
  In Nature's own revealing!
Wherever summer's grass is green,
  Or winter's snows are hoary,
We see Thee, though Thou art unseen;
  We know Thee by Thy glory!

5 We linger in our parting song;
  We praise Thee as we sever;—
The summer days will not be long,
  Ere we shall praise forever!
All hail! then, for the Summer Land
  Whose blossoms never wither;—
Though here we part each other's hand,
  We keep our journey thither!

RURAL FESTIVAL.

L. M.   **85.**   *James Lombard.

" Let all the trees of the wood rejoice."

1 While here, beneath the trees, we meet,
   To spend the day 'mid fields and flowers,
May every heart with gladness beat,
   Through all these golden summer hours.

2 Bright sunbeams through the branches glance,
   The leaves make music in the breeze,
And why should we not sing and dance
   In joyous harmony with these?

3 And while we pause with awe to read
   The lessons of the earth and sky,
May we drink in that blessed creed—
   That God to us is ever nigh!

4 Full faith in God, and hearts to do
   The work that He in love has given,
Will make the world we journey through,
   The way of light and bliss to Heaven!

86.   *C. T. Brooks.

" All the trees of the field clap their hands."
                       Air—" Sunset Tree."

1   Come, come, come!
Come, parents, teachers, friends,
   And join our grateful lay;
God in His goodness sends
   A holy joy to-day.
The Summer hours are o'er —
   The sultry summer days
And autumn comes once more
   With its swelling voice of praise.
           Come, come, come!

2   Come, come, come!
Come, loved ones, gather round
   With a glad and sacred lay,
For this is holy ground
   Your footsteps press to-day.
God's hand hath decked this green
   Rich carpet of the sod;
And smiling o'er the scene
   Is the calm, blue eye of God.
                Come, come, come!

3   Come, come, come!
Come, and with songs of praise
   Thank Him who kindly came
To bid all nature's ways
   A God of Love proclaim.
And when His smile above
   Ye seek your homes of rest,
Pray that a Father's love
   May dwell in every breast.
                Come, come, come!

C. M.   **87.**   *GRACE GREENWOOD.

" Let the heavens rejoice, and let the earth be glad."

1 The pleasant winds are out at play
   Among the forest bowers,
The wild birds flit from spray to spray,
   The turf laughs out in flowers;

2 The bee, with happy, murmurous song,
   Pursues his sweet employ,—
Gay insects float the air along,
   In living shapes of joy;

3 The stream goes singing through the wood,
  The green leaves dance on high,
  The lovely clouds above us brood,
  White isles in deeps of sky;

4 To perfumed shades, from bloomy sod, ˙
  The soul of gladness calls,
  And o'er us, like the smile of God,
  The tender sunlight falls.

5 Since naught in earth or heaven looks sad,
  Oh, Father, shall not we,
  Thy little children dear, be glad
  In life, in love, in Thee?

6 Then gracious Lord, deign Thou to bless
  Our mirth, our joyous plays, —
  Accept our simple happiness
  As gratitude and praise!

C. M. 61   **88.**   *Grace Greenwood.

" Let the field be joyful, and all that therein is."

1 Our dear Lord Jesus, thou didst call
  Young children once to Thee,
  Didst hold them in thy loving arms,
  And bless them tenderly, —
  Now, like those children, let us come
  And gather round thy knee.

2 Oh, teach us that God dwelleth here!—
  These woods His leafy shrines —
  That incense rises from the flowers,
  And fragrant swinging vines,
  And wordless psalms swell up from out
  The solemn sounding pines.

3 Oh, teach us to behold, where'er
   Our joyous footsteps rove,
The emblems of a Father's care,
   And tokens of His love,
In sunshine smiling on the sward—
   In clouds that brood above.

4 His glory in the golden morn,
   His peace in noon's repose,
His goodness in the twilight's shades
   That softly round us close —
" The beauty of His holiness"
   In every wilding rose!

5 Oh, hear our hymns, and bless our feast,
   And smile upon our play,—
Oh, fill our hearts with thy dear love,
   And keep us glad and gay,
And sinless as the little birds,
   Throughout this summer day.

L M.   **89.**   *JAMES LOMBARD.

" The day goeth away."

1 See how the sun, declining, fills
   The forest with a golden glow!
It lingers on the distant hills,
   As though the light were loth to go.

2 But beams of lovelier light than this,
   Are shining now within our hearts,—
'Tis seen in looks and smiles of bliss,
   That soften as the day departs.

3 And as we see the shadows fall,
   That tell us soon the night will come,
We heed them as the silent call
   To leave these scenes, and journey home.

4 Good night! To every happy heart,
    May dreams of all things bright be given,
And every day, like this, impart
    A glimpse of fairer ones in heaven.

5 So, when the last Good Night is said,
    And God's good angel whispers, "Come!"
That voice shall peace and comfort shed,
    And be the call for "going home!"

8's & 7's M. 6 l.   **90.**   Mrs. S. C E. Mayo.

"The shadows of the evening are stretched out."

1 Hark! the solemn pines are sighing
    High above us in the breeze;
And our strains are softly dying
    Far away amid the trees;
Lengthening shadows, too, are flying
    All along the verdant leas.

2 Let our spirits, lowly kneeling,
    Lift their reverential praise,
With a deep and fervent feeling
    To Thee, Guardian of our days;
Thou, who ever art revealing
    Some new wonder in Thy ways.

3 Holiest! Truest! Best! Divinest!
    On Thy sacred name we call;
Thou, who in yon azure shinest,
    Where the stars before Thee fall;
Thou, who in each leaf enshrinest
    Tokens of Thy love to all!

4 Bless us, while around this altar,
    We with mingling spirits bend;
Be each heart a written psalter,
    Where all sacred notes may blend
In sweet praise, that ne'er shall falter,
    Throughout worlds that never end!

ANNIVERSARY.

8's & 7's M.   **91.** WILLIS GAYLORD CLARK.

" The Lord shall be thy confidence."

1 We have met in peace together,
   In the house of God again:
 Constant friends have lead us hither,
   Here to chant the joyous strain;
 Here to breathe our adoration,
   While the balmy breeze of Spring,
 Like the Spirit of Salvation,
   Comes with gladness on His wing!

2 We have met, and time is flying,
   We shall part — and still his wing,
 Sweeping o'er the dead and dying,
   Will the changeful seasons bring:
 Let us, while our hearts are lightest,
   In our fresh and early years,
 Turn to Him whose smile is brightest,
   And whose grace will calm our fears.

3 He will aid us, though existence
   With its sorrows wound the breast;
 Shining in the onward distance,
   Faith will mark the Land of Rest:
 There, 'mid day-beams round Him playing,
   We our Father's face shall see,
 And shall hear Him gently saying,
   " Little children, come to me!"

L. M. 6 l.   **92.**   *MRS. H. J. LEWIS

" Bring an offering and come into His courts."

1 We bring, O God, no gift of flowers,
   No costly gems to deck Thy shrine;
 But Father, with our dawning powers,
   We come to praise Thy love divine:

Not Persia's fragrant rose could be
So sweet an offering, Lord to Thee.

2 We thank Thee that Thy courts we tread,
   And that we here Thy name may sing!
No gold and pearls before Thee spread
   That boasting earthly pride could bring
From rayless mine, or ocean's floor,
Would add one treasure to Thy store.

3 The heaving sea, the lonely star,
   The mountain high, the stream and hill,
All that we have, and all we are,
   Are gifts of Thy most gracious will:
And Oh, the love Thy Son that gave,
To die, our souls from sin to save!

4 Father divine! with glad acclaim
   Our feeble voices now would blend,
To praise anew Thy hallowed name,
   Through Jesus Christ, our Guide and Friend:
And may he lead us home to Thee
When death shall set our spirits free!

8's & 7's M.   **93.**   *Mrs. C. M. Sawyer.

" And other sheep I have, which are not of this fold; them
also I must bring, and they shall hear my voice."

1 Father, Thou who art in Heaven,
   O'er us brood in love to-day;
Let Thy truth our spirits leaven,
   While our young lips sing and pray,
Gathered in Thy holy temple,
   Lo! a thousand hearts we bow!
By Thy loving, pure example,
   Saviour, King, inspire us now!

2 Make our love deep, true, out-reaching,
   Clasping all, where'er they be ;
Make our lives, like angels' preaching,
   Strong to lead the lost to Thee !
Oh, the thousand streets and alleys —
   Oh, the islands far away —
Oh, the countless hills and valleys,
   Where they know not Thee to-day !

3 Shall they walk, thus blindly, groping,
   Down the paths of sin and death ?
Shall they, like dumb brutes, unhoping,
   'Mid the darkness yield their breath ?
What to them though Thou, in Zion,
   On the cross hast bled and died,
If they know not that, in dying,
   Thou for them wert crucified ?

4 Yes ! we know, though long averted,
   Father, though Thine eyes may be,
Never yet was one deserted,
   Ne'er will one be lost by Thee !
Peace, our hearts ! Oh, triumph rather,
   Of this last great solace sure,
In thine own good time, oh, Father,
   Every ill will find a cure !

8's & 7's M.   **94.**   *Mrs. C. M. Sawyer.

"And there shall be one fold, and one Shepherd."

1 We have sung the songs of gladness,
   We have lisped the words of prayer,
But a sudden cloud of sadness
   Seems to darken all the air ;
We remember there are others
   Who our prayers to-day should claim,
Who, though born of Christian mothers,
   Never heard the Saviour's name.

2 Yes! in foul, polluted cellars,
   And in dens without a name,
There are sin-benighted dwellers,
   Lying down in guilt and shame.
O, the savage in his highlands,
   And the heathen in his lairs,
In the far-off tropic islands,
   See a holier light than theirs.

3 Faithful teachers, who have led us,
   Where the love of God is rife —
Christian preachers, who have fed us
   With the sacred bread of life :
Ye who send your vessels, freighted
   Where the dark-browed heathen roam,
Till the teeming isles are sated, —
   Shall they starve for light at home ?

4 Father, may Love's morning, breaking.
   Soon around them all be fair ;
For our hearts within are aching
   At the heavy woes they bear.
O, ye young, but blind immortals,
   You shall not for ever sin ;
Wide, oh, wide are Heaven's portals,
   And you yet shall enter in !

L. M.   **95.**   *James Lombard.

" While the evil days come not."

1 We'come ere yet the ills of life
   Have cast their shadows o'er our way,
For strength to conquer mid the strife,
   And bear the burden of the day.

2 Whate'er our lot in life may be,
   May we its duties well perform,
And still thy goodness, Father see
   Alike in sunshine and in storm.

3 May we our faithful teachers aid,
  And grant that in their labors high,
They be not weary nor dismayed,
  Ere yet the harvest-time draws nigh.

4 And while within these walls we meet,
  To gather words of wisdom here,
May kindly deeds and converse sweet,
  Bind every heart in love sincere.

NATIONAL ANNIVERSARY.

96.   *MRS. C. M. SAWYER.

" Our fathers trusted in Thee: And Thou didst deliver
them."

Air—"Star-Spangled Banner."

1 All hail to the day when our fathers arose,
  The rod and the sceptre of tyranny scorning,
And proudly defying the might of their foes,
  Proclaimed to the nation that Freedom was dawning!
When they sternly awoke to their wrongs, and the yoke
Of the haughty oppressor indignantly broke!
Let the long shout roll on, till the sound dies away
O'er the far distant mountains—*All hail to the day!*

2 O, long may we cherish the deeds and the fame
  Of the sires who their all for our liberty plighted,
And in our young hearts may the patriot flame
  Which burned in their bosoms so purely, be lighted!
And still green be the thought of the lessons they taught,
When 'mid toils and 'mid dangers our freedom they bought!
Let the shout thunder on till the sound dies away
O'er the far distant mountains—*All hail to the day!*

3 The time will soon come when, in silence and dust
  Our fathers' strong arms will together be blended;
To whom, then. but us, can they yield up their trust?
  By whose arms, but our own, will the prize be defended!
Then still bright be the fires. that were lit by our sires
Upon Freedom's high altar till nature expires!
Let the shout still roll on, till the sound dies away
O'er the far distant mountains—*All hail to the day!*

4 We will move on our way undismayed by the world,
  And pray that the smile of the Lord may attend us:
For the Just and the True if our flag be unfurled,
  His Right Hand the Great God of Battles will lend us.
Let our hearts then be steeled, and our arms never yield,
  And the Lord God of Hosts be our sword and our shield;
While the shout still rolls on, till the sound dies away
O'er the far distant mountains— *All hail to the day!*

7's & 6's M. **97.**

" The Lord our God be with us as He was with our fathers.'

1 We come, with joy and gladness,
    To breathe our songs of praise,
  Nor let one note of sadness
    Be mingled in our lays ;
  For 't is a hallowed story,
    This theme of freedom's birth:
  Our fathers' deeds of glory
    Are echoed round the earth.

2 The sound is waxing stronger,
    And thrones and nations hear—
  Proud men shall rule no longer,
    For God the Lord is near :
  And He will crush oppression,
    And raise the humble mind,
  And give the earth's possession
    Among the good and kind.

3 And then shall sink the mountains,
    Where pride and power are crowned,
  And peace, like gentle fountains,
    Shall shed its blessing round.
  O God! we would adore Thee,
    And in Thy shadow rest;
  Our fathers bowed before Thee,
    And trusted, and were blest.

6's & 4's M.   **98.**

" Thou in mercy hast led forth the people which Thou hast redeemed."

1 My country ! 'tis of thee,
Sweet land of liberty —
    Of thee I sing ;
Land where my fathers died !
Land of the pilgrim's pride !
From every mountain-side
    Let freedom ring.

2 My native country ! thee —
Land of the blest and free —
    Thy name I love ;
I love thy rocks and rills,
Thy woods and templed hills,
My heart with rapture thrills,
    Like that above.

3 Let music swell the breeze,
And ring from all the trees
    Sweet freedom's song ;
Let mortal tongues awake,
Let all that breathe partake,
Let rocks their silence break,
    The sound prolong.

4 Our fathers' God ! to Thee —
Thou who hast made us free !
    To Thee we sing ;
Long may our land be bright
With freedom's holy light ;
Protect us by Thy might,
    Great God, our King !

L. M.   **99.**   J. G. WHITTIER.

"Relieve the oppressed."

1 O Thou, whose presence went before
   Our fathers in their weary way,
As with Thy chosen moved of yore
   The fire by night, the cloud by day!

2 When, from each temple of the free,
   A nation's song ascends to heaven,
Most holy Father, unto Thee,
   Now let our humble prayer be given.

3 And grant, O Father, that the time
   Of earth's deliverance may be near,
When every land, and tongue, and clime,
   The message of Thy love shall hear;

4 When, smitten as with fire from heaven,
   The captive's chain shall sink in dust,
And to his fettered soul be given
   The glorious freedom of the just!

THE LAW OF LOVE.

C. M.   **100.**

" Be kindly affectioned one to another."

1 A little word in kindness said,
   A motion, or a tear,
Has often healed the heart that's bled,
   And made a friend sincere.

2 A word, a look, has crushed to earth
   Full oft a budding flower:
Which, had a smile but owned its birth,
   Would bless life's darkest hour.

3 Then deem it not an idle thing
  A pleasant word to speak ;
The face you wear, the thoughts you bring,
  A heart may heal or break.

C. M. **101.** William Cutter.

" For who hath despised the day of small things?"

1 What if each little drop should plead,
  So small a thing as I
Can ne'er refresh the thirsty mead,
  I'll tarry in the sky ?

2 What if each shining beam of noon
  Should in its fountain stay,
Because its feeble light alone
  Cannot create a day ?

3 Doth not each rain-drop help to form
  The cool, refreshing shower?
And every ray of light to warm
  And beautify the flower?

4 'Tis thus the good each child may do,
  When many do their best,
Will help to bring within our view
  The glory of the blest.

6's & 5's M. **102.** Mrs. Julia A. Carney.

" Here a little and there a little."

1 Little drops of water,
    Little grains of sand,
  Make the mighty ocean,
    And the beauteous land.

2 And the little moments,
    Humble though they be,
  Make the mighty ages
    Of eternity.

3 So our little errors
  Lead the soul away
From the path of virtue,
  Oft in sin to stray.

4 Little deeds of kindness,
  Little words of love,
Make our earth an Eden,
  Like the heaven above.

5 Little seeds of mercy,
  Sown by youthful hands,
Grow to bless the nations,
  Far in heathen lands.

C. M. **103.** MRS. JULIA A. CARNEY.

" If ye forgive men their trespasses, your heavenly Father
will also forgive you."

1 Think gently of the erring one!
  O do not thou forget,
However darkly stained by sin,
  He is thy brother yet!

2 Speak gently to the erring one!
  Thou yet mayst win him back,
With holy words, and tones of love,
  To virtue's pleasant track!

3 Forget not thou hast often sinned,
  And sinful yet may be: •
Deal gently with the erring heart,
  As God has dealt with thee!

C. M.   **104.**

"Speaking the truth in love."

1 Speak gently—it is better far
    To rule by love than fear;
  Speak gently — let no harsh word mar
    The good we might do here.

2 Speak gently to the young — for they
    Will have enough to bear;
  Pass through this life as best they may,
    'Tis full of anxious care.

3 Speak gently to the aged one,
    Grieve not the care-worn heart;
  The sands of life are nearly run,
    Let them in peace depart.

4 Speak gently—'tis a little thing
    Dropped in the heart's deep well;
  The good, the joy that it may bring,
    Eternity shall tell!

CONSECRATION OF A CHAPEL OR VESTRY.

L. M.   **105.**   *JAMES LOMBARD.

"This is none other but the house of God."

1 Lord! in Thy sight completed stands
    This temple to Thy truth and grace;
  And now we lift our hearts and hands
    To Thee, to consecrate the place!

2 May all by whom these courts are trod,
    Who here shall pray to be forgiven,
  Find this indeed the house of God,
    And this the very gate of Heaven.

3 Lord ! in our hearts Thy kingdom build,
  That they may living temples be;
That, with Thy faith and comfort filled,
  We may each day live nearer Thee.

4 And when at last shall break the bands
  That bind our spirits to the dust,
To Thine own house, not made with hands,
  Take us to dwell with all the just.

THE WAY OF LIFE.

7's M.   **106.**   *Mary Noel Meigs.

" O Lord, teach me Thy paths."

1 Little travellers, on the road,
  Leading up to God's abode,
  Watch each footstep, lest ye stray
  From the safe and narrow way.

2 Wily arts the Tempter hath,
  To allure you from the path;
  Many a shining bait he holds,
  To ensnare unwary souls.

3 Little travellers, keep the way,
  Watching, lest ye go astray;
  Safe and pleasant is the road
  Leading up to Heaven and God !

107.   *Mrs. C. M. Sawyer.

"Lead me and guide me."

Air—" Believe me, if all those endearing young charms."

1 This life is a journey, and widely diverge
  The pathways our feet must pursue;
And many and wily the tempters that urge
  To depart from the good and the true.

Too oft we give ear,—in our folly and pride,
  We the brink of the precipice dare,
Though the voice of an angel is heard at our side,
  Ever tenderly pleading, "Beware!"

2 Our Father in Heaven! lest we should forget
    That our souls, in Thine own image formed,
  Though upon them eternity's seal Thou hast set,
    May be darkened, and shrunk, and deformed,
  We bring them to Thee, ere their whiteness departs,
    Or the world has polluted their truth;
  We kneel at Thine altar, and give Thee our hearts,
    While each pulse is still bounding with youth.

3 We know that whatever our fortunes may be,
    Or wherever our lots may be cast,
  Tho' false prove the world, if we cling but to *Thee*,
    Thou, O God, wilt be true to the last!
  Then, in life's radiant morn, in its soberer noon,
    In its tottering years of decay,
  Our Father, but grant this one infinite boon,—
    Be *Thou* ever our guide and our stay!

L. M.   **108.**   L. E. LANDON.

"Train up a child in the way he should go."

1 While yet the youthful spirit bears
    The image of its God within,
  And uneffaced that beauty wears,
    Which may too soon be stained by sin:

2 Then is the time for faith and love
    To take in charge their precious care,—
  Teach the young heart to look above,
    Teach the young knee to bend in prayer.

3 The world will come with care and crime,
    And tempt too oft the heart astray;
  Still, the seed sown in early time,
    Shall not be wholly cast away.

4 The infant prayer, the infant hymn,
   Within the darkened soul will rise,
When age's weary eye is dim,
   And the grave's shadow round us lies.

5 Lord, grant our hearts be so inclined
   Thy work to seek, Thy will to do,
And while we teach the youthful mind,
   Our own be taught Thy lessons too.

MISCELLANEOUS.

C. M.   **109.**   JONES VERY.

" As ye sow, so shall ye reap."

1 The bud will soon become a flower,
   The flower become a seed;
Then seize, O youth! the present hour—
   Of that thou hast most need.

2 Do thy best always — do it now,—
   For, in the present time,
As in the furrows of a plough,
   Fall seeds of good or crime.

3 The sun and rain will ripen fast
   Each seed that thou hast sown;
And every act and word at last
   By its own fruit be known.

4 And soon the harvest of thy toil
   Rejoicing thou shalt reap;
Or o'er thy wild, neglected soil,
   Go forth in shame to weep!

7's & 5's M.   **110.**

"I must work the works of Him that sent me, while it is day."

1 Pluck the rose while now it blooms,
   Now 'tis fresh and bright;
Wait not till to-morrow comes —
   Time is swift in flight.

2 Do thy deeds of kindness now,
   Ere to-morrow's light;
What may chance thou canst not know,
   Time is swift in flight.

3 Wouldst thou true enjoyment find?
   Now do what is right;
Ever bearing in thy mind,
   Time is swift in flight.

7's & 8's M.   **111.**

"He that walketh uprightly, walketh surely."

1 He who walks in virtue's way,
   Firm and fearless, walketh surely;
Constant ever, while 'tis day,
   On he speeds, and speeds securely.

2 Flowers of peace beneath him grow,
   Suns of pleasure brighten o'er him;
Memory's joys behind him go,
   Hope's sweet angels fly before him.

3 Thus he moves from stage to stage,
   Smiles of earth and heaven attending;
Softly sinking down in age,
   And at last to death descending

4 Cradled in its quiet deep,
 Calm as summer's loveliest even,
 He shall sleep the hallowed sleep;
 Sleep whose waking is in Heaven.

7's M.

112.

"Thy word have I hid in my heart,"

1 Holy Bible! book divine!
 Precious treasure! thou art mine!
 Mine to tell me whence I came;
 Mine to tell me what I am;

2 Mine to chide me when I rove;
 Mine to show a Father's love;
 Mine to guide my wayward feet;
 Mine to judge, condemn, acquit;

3 Mine to comfort in distress;
 Mine to cheer, sustain, and bless;
 Mine to show by living faith,
 How to triumph over death;

4 Mine to tell of joys to come;
 Mine to lead the spirit home:
 O thou precious book divine
 Holy Bible! thou art mine!

6 & 5's M.

113.

" The Winter is over and gone."

1 Summer days are coming,
 Winter days are gone;
 Merry birds are singing
 In the flowery lawn.

2 Now the sun is shining,
 With his cheerful rays;
 O how very pleasant
 Are these summer days!

3 Honey-bees are gathering
　　Sweets from all the flowers;
Ever, ever busy,
　　All the sunny hours.

4 May we learn the lesson
　　To be busy too;
Ever, ever seeking
　　Useful work to do.

5 God, our great Creator,
　　Gave these summer days;
May our hearts and voices
　　Join to give Him praise!

C. M.

114.

Mary Howitt.

"Consider the lilies of the field."

1 God might have made the earth bring forth
　　Enough for great and small:
The oak tree and the cedar tree,
　　Without a flower at all.

2 We might have had enough, enough
　　For every want of ours;
For luxury, medicine and toil,
　　And yet have had no flowers.

3 Then, wherefore, wherefore were they made,
　　All dyed with rainbow light?
All fashioned with supremest grace,
　　Upspringing day and night?

4 Our outward life requires them not;
　　Then wherefore had they birth?
To minister delight to man —
　　To beautify the earth;

5 To comfort man; to whisper hope,
    Whene'er his faith is dim;
For He who careth for the flowers,
    Will much more care for him!

6's M.   **115.**   G. W. BETHUNE, D. D.

"Your heavenly Father feedeth them."

1 Spare, spare the gentle bird,
    Nor do the warbler wrong;
In the green wood is heard
    Its sweet and gentle song.

2 Its song so sweet and glad,
    Each listener's heart has stirred,
And none, however sad,
    But blessed that happy bird.

3 Oh, laugh not at my words,
    Which warn your childhood's hours;
Cherish the gentle birds,
    Cherish the fragile flowers.

4 For since man was bereft
    Of Paradise, in tears,
God the sweet things has left
    To cheer our eyes and ears.

C. M.   **116.**   *MRS. C. M. SAWYER.

"Are ye not much better than they?"

1 The birds that speed their fearless flight,
    When Northern hills grow bleak,
To lands whose skies are always bright,
    A warmer home to seek:

2 With tireless wing and steady eye,
   Their journey still pursue,
For God, along the darkest sky,
   Conducts them safely through!

3 O, if the wild-bird keeps the way
   Thus marked by God for her,
Nor starless night, nor sunless day,
   Can lead her flight to err : ·

4 Shall we, around whose restless feet
   A light diviner falls,
Like blind men wandering in the street,
   Turn where each tempter calls ?

5 No! Father, No! or if our soul
   Perchance awhile should stray,
The wild-bird, winging to its goal,
   Shall teach a better way!

6's & 5's M.   **117.**   *JAMES LOMBARD.

" Lay up for yourselves treasures in Heaven."

 1 Things we love and cherish,
   In their beauty perish,
     Change is on them all :
   To the fondest, dearest,
   Death is ever nearest,
     With his sable pall.

 2 Life is but a flower,
   Blooming for an hour;
     Soon to fade away;
   Everything is fleeting,
   Every heart is beating,
     Feebler day by day.

3 There are fadeless treasures,
  Yielding sweetest pleasures,
    Nothing can destroy :
  But the seeking spirit,
  Only can inherit
    Such immortal joy !

4 Now, in life's bright morning,
  Every folly scorning,
    Let us choose the right :
  Then, whate'er betide us,
  God will ever guide us,
    Where the way is bright.

C. H. M   **118.**

" What is your life ?"

1 O, what is life ? 'Tis like a flower
  That blooms at early dawn ;
We see it flourish for an hour,
  And then we find it gone ;
For death soon comes,—a wintry day,
And bears the lovely flower away.

2 O, what is life ? 'Tis like the bow
  That spans the arch on high ;
We love to see its colors glow,
  But, while we gaze, they die :
Life fades as soon,—'tis here to-day,
To-morrow it may pass away.

3 Lord, what is life ? If spent with Thee
  In duty, praise and prayer,
How long or short our life may be
  We shall be in Thy care :
And though life fade, our joys shall last
When life and all its joys are past.

7's & 6's P. M.   **119.**

"It is even a vapor, that appeareth for a little time, and then vanisheth away."

1 Time is winging us away
    To our eternal home;
  Life is but a little day,—
    A journey to the tomb;
  Youth and vigor soon will fade,
    Blooming beauty lose its charms,
  And this mortal frame be laid
    To rest in death's cold arms.

2 Time is winging us away
    To our eternal home;
  Life is but a little day,—
    A journey to the tomb;
  But the spirit shall enjoy
    Health and beauty soon above,
  Where no earthly griefs annoy,
    Safe in the Father's love.

7's M.   **120.**   *C. T. BROOKS.

"Keep thy heart with all diligence."

1 O my heart! from thee, from thee,
  Wells the fount of life for me;
  And when thou true peace hast found,
  Peace and beauty reign around.

2 Love thy Maker—with him walk,
  And with Him hold friendly talk,
  In the morning's kindling flush,
  Noontide's glow, and evening's hush.

3 Love thy brother—God's own child!
  With pure love and undefiled!
  Stained with vice or steeped in sin,
  O, let Pity take him in!

4 Love all creatures in His name
From whose love all being came,
And, through life and nature trace
Every where His will and grace.

5 Then, my heart, Thy peace shall be
Like a stream that, full and free,
Nourished by the Heavenly wells,
On toward heaven's broad ocean swells!

6's & 5's M. **121.** *THEODORE TILTON.

"They shall run and not be weary."

1 Take thy staff, O pilgrim!
Haste thee on thy way;
Let the morrow find thee
Farther than to-day.
If thou seek the city
Of the Golden Street,
Pause not on thy pathway,
Rest not weary feet.

2 In the heavenly journey
Press with zeal along—
Resting will but weary,
Running make thee strong.
Wings that eagles carry,
Rear them in their flight;
So thy burden bears thee—
Surely then 'tis light!

3 Haste, it hath been told thee—
All things are thine own;
Pass the pearly portals,
Stand before the throne.
Here thy journey endeth,
Here thy staff lay down,
Enter here thy mansion,
Here receive thy crown!

7's & 6's M.   **122.**

"He shall speak peace unto the heathen."

1 From Greenland's icy mountains,
   From India's coral strand,
Where Afric's sunny fountains
   Roll down their golden sands;
From many an ancient river,
   From many a palmy plain,
They call us to deliver
   Their land from error's chain.

2 What though the spicy breezes
   Blow soft o'er Ceylon's isle;
Though every prospect pleases,
   And only man is vile;
In vain with lavish kindness
   The gifts of God are strown;
The heathen, in his blindness,
   Bows down to wood and stone.

3 Shall we, whose souls are lighted
   By wisdom from on high—
Shall we to men benighted
   The lamp of life deny?
Salvation! O, Salvation!
   The joyful sound proclaim,
Till earth's remotest nation
   Has learned Messiah's name.

6's & 5's M.   **123.**   *JAMES LOMBARD.

"Get wisdom, get understanding."

1 Gladly now in childhood,
   Do we sing and play,
Free as in the wildwood,
   Are the birds in May;

But a sweeter pleasure
  We in study find ;
Here there is a treasure
  Lasting as the mind.

2 Soft the sunlight falleth,
    On the opening blooms ;
  From their hearts it calleth,
    Mildest of perfumes :
  Sweeter light is given
    To the earnest soul,
  That hath nobly striven
    For a pure control.

3 Let us wisely treasure
    Life's unfading flowers,
  Then the richest pleasure
    Shall be ever ours :
  And if we are lowly,
    Acting well our parts,
  Nought but feelings holy
    Then shall rule our hearts.

CONCLUDING.

7's M. **124.**

" I was glad when they said, Let us go into the house of the Lord."

1 To Thy temple I repair ;
  Lord, I love to worship there ;
  Abba ! Father ! give me grace
  In Thy courts to seek Thy face.

2 While Thy glorious praise is sung,
  Touch my lips, unloose my tongue ;
  While the prayers of saints ascend,
  God of love, to mine attend.

3 While Thy ministers proclaim
   Peace and pardon in Thy name,
While I hearken to Thy law,
   Fill my soul with humble awe.

4 From Thy house when I return,
   May my heart within me burn;
And, at evening, let me say,
   "I have walked with God to-day."

8's & 7's M.   **125.**

"Now the God of peace be with you all."

1 Lord, dismiss us with Thy blessing,
   Hope and comfort from above;
Let us each, Thy peace possessing,
   Triumph in redeeming love.

2 Thanks we give, and adoration,
   For Thy Gospel's joyful sound;
May the fruits of Thy salvation
   In our hearts and lives abound.

3 Make us gentle, kind, and lowly,
   Teach us, Father, from Thy word,
How we may be good and holy,
   Like to Jesus Christ our Lord.

8's & 7's M.   **126.**   *Mrs. C. M. Sawyer.

"Let the peace of God rule in your hearts."

1 We have met—and gladness round us
   Hath a band of beauty twined;
Love, with genial smile hath bound us
   Heart to heart, and mind to mind.
Words of friendship have been spoken,
   Hands been clasped, ne'er clasped before;
Be the friendship long unbroken,
   Though the hands be clasped no more!

2 We are parting—softly breathe it—
  Every low, and farewell tone!
That each heart may catch and wreath it
  With the gems it calls its own;
True hands, in each other pressing—
  Moistened eye and lingering heart—
Lips invoking God's rich blessing —
  Thus, O friends! thus let us part.

7's M. **127.** *W. C. BRYANT.

"The Lord lift up His countenance upon Thee, and give thee peace."

1 When this song of praise shall cease,
  Let Thy servants, Lord, depart,
With the blessing of Thy peace,
  And Thy love, in every heart.

2 Oh, where'er our path may lie,
  Father, let us not forget
That we walk beneath Thine eye,
  That Thy care upholds us yet.

3 Blind are we, and weak and frail;
  Be Thine aid forever near;
May the fear to sin prevail
  Over every other fear.

8's & 7's M. **128.**

"The Lord bless thee, and keep thee."

1 Father! grant us now Thy blessing,
  Smile upon us from above;
Let us all, pure hearts possessing,
  Fill our lives with deeds of love.

2 Make us gentle, kind and lowly;
  Teach us, Father, by Thy word,
How we may be good and holy,
  Like to Jesus Christ, our Lord.

8's & 7's M. **129.**

"The Lord make IIis face to shine upon thee, and be gracious unto thee."

1 God of our salvation, hear us;
  Bless, O bless us, ere we go;
When we join the world, be near us,
  Lest we cold and careless grow:
    Saviour, keep us —
  Keep us safe from every foe.

2 As our steps are drawing nearer
  To our everlasting home,
May our view of heaven grow clearer,
  Hope more bright of joys to come;
    And, when dying,
  May Thy presence cheer the gloom.

6's & 5's M. **130.**

"After this manner therefore pray ye."

1 Our Father in heaven,
  We hallow Thy name;
May Thy kingdom holy
  On earth be the same!
O give to us daily
  Our portion of bread;
It is from Thy bounty
  That all must be fed.

2 Forgive our transgressions,
  And teach us to know
That humble compassion
  That pardons each foe :
Keep us from temptation,
  From weakness and sin,
And Thine be the glory,
  Forever — Amen.

L. M.   131.

"Let every thing that hath breath praise the Lord."

1 From all that dwell below the skies,
Let the Creator's praise arise;
Let the Redeemer's name be sung,
Through every land, by every tongue.

2 Eternal are Thy mercies, Lord,
Eternal truth attends Thy word :
Thy praise shall sound from shore to shore,
Till suns shall rise and set no more.

CHANTS.

I.—VENITE, EXULTEMUS.

O come, let us sing un | to the | Lord ‖ let us heartily rejoice in the | strength of | our sal | vation.

Let us come before His presence | with thanks- | giving ‖ and show ourselves | glad in | Him with | psalms.

For the Lord is a | great | God ‖ and a great | King a | bove all | gods.

In His hand are all the corners | of the | earth ‖ and the strength of the | hills is | His | also.

The sea is His | and He | made it ‖ and His hands pre | pared the | dry | land.

O come, let us worship | and fall | down ‖ and kneel be | fore the | Lord our | Maker,

For He is the | Lord our | God ‖ and we are the people of His pasture, | and the | sheep of His | hand.

O worship the Lord in the | beauty of | holiness ‖ let the whole earth | stand in | awe of | Him.

For He cometh, for He cometh to | judge the | earth ‖ and with righteousness to judge the world and the | people | with His | truth.

II.—JUBILATE.

Psalm c.

O be joyful in the Lord, | all ye | lands ‖ serve the Lord with gladness, and come before His | presence | with a | song.

Be ye sure that the Lord | He is | God ‖ it is He that hath made us, and not we ourselves; we are His people, | and the | sheep of His | pasture.

O go your way into His gates with thanksgiving, and into His | courts with | praise ‖ be thankful unto Him, and speak | good | of His | Name.

For the Lord is gracious, His mercy is | ever- | lasting ‖ and His truth endureth from gener | ation to | gener | ation.

III.—Cantate Domino.

Psalm xcviii.

O sing unto the Lord a | new | song ‖ for He hath | done | marvellous | things.

With His own right hand, and with His | holy | arm ‖ hath He | gotten Him | self the | victory.

The Lord declared | His sal | vation ‖ His righteousness hath He openly showed | in the | sight of the | heathen.

He hath remembered His mercy and truth toward the | house of | Israel ‖ and all the ends of the world have seen the sal | vation | of our | God.

Show yourselves joyful unto the Lord, | all ye | lands ‖ sing, re | joice, | and give | thanks.

Praise the Lord up | on the | harp ‖ sing to the | harp with a | psalm of | thanksgiving.

With trumpets | also and | shawms ‖ O show yourselves joyful be | fore the | Lord, the | King.

Let the sea make a noise, and all that | therein | is ‖ the round world, and | they that | dwell there | in.

Let the floods clap their hands, and let the hills be joyful together be | fore the | Lord ‖ for He | cometh to | judge the | earth.

With righteousness shall He | judge the | world ‖ and the | people | with | equity.

IV.—Bonum est Confiteri.

Psalm xcii.

It is a good thing to give thanks un | to the | Lord ‖ and to sing praises unto Thy | Name, | O Most | Highest;

To tell of Thy loving-kindness early | in the | morning ‖ and of Thy truth | in the | night- | season;

Upon an instrument of ten strings, and up | on the | lute ‖ upon a loud instrument, | and up | on the | harp.

For Thou, Lord, hast made me glad | through Thy | works ‖ and I will rejoice in giving praise for the oper | ations | of Thy | hands.

V.—Deus Misereatur.

Psaim lxvii.

God be merciful unto us, | and | bless us ‖ and show us the light of His countenance, and be | merciful | unto | us;

That Thy way may be | known upon | earth ‖ Thy saving | health a | mong all | nations.

Let the people praise | Thee, O | God ‖ yea, let | all the | people | praise Thee.

O let the nations rejoice | and be | glad ‖ for Thou shalt judge the folk righteously, and govern the | nations | upon | earth.

Let the people praise | Thee, O | God ‖ yea, let | all the | people | praise Thee.

Then shall the earth bring | forth her | increase ‖ and God, even our own God, shall | give | us His | blessing.

God | shall | bless us ‖ and all the ends | of the | world shall | love Him.

VI.—Benedic, anima mea.

Psalm ciii.

Praise the Lord, | O my | soul || and all that is within me, | praise His | holy | Name.

Praise the Lord, | O my | soul || and for | get not | all His | benefits;

Who forgiveth | all thy | sin || and healeth | all | thine in | firmities ;

Who saveth thy life | from de | struction || and crowneth thee with | mercy and | loving | kindness.

O praise the Lord, ye Angels of His, ye that ex- | cel in | strength || ye that fulfil His commandment, and hearken unto the | voice | of His | word.

O praise the Lord, all | ye His | hosts || ye servants of | His that | do His | pleasure.

O speak good of the Lord, all ye works of His, in all places of | His do | minion || praise thou the | Lord, | O my | soul.